DON'T GO
BACK
TO
SLEEP

a Memoir as a Meditation

D. Gregory Futch, M.Div

Don't Go Back to Sleep: A Memoir as Meditation
Copyright © 2021 by D. Greg Futch

All rights reserved. No part of this publication may be reproduced or transmitted in any form or by any means, electronic or mechanical, including photocopy, recording, or any information storage and retrieval system without express permission in writing from the publisher.

Many thanks to the following for permissions to use:
1. Coleman Barks, Rumi quote as epigraph at front of book, *The Essential Rumi*, p. 36; Harper San Francisco, 1995; 2. Wendell Berry, quote from *Our Only World*, p. 111; Counterpoint, Berkeley, 2015; 3. Ibn Arabi, quote from *Kernel of the Kernel*, by Ismail Hakki Bursevi, translated by Bulent Rauf; Beshara Publications, 2016; 4. Ramakrishna, quote from *Sayings of Sri Ramakrishna*, p. 149, Sri Ramakrishna Math, Chennai, 1971; 5. Wayne Teasdale, quote from *The Mystic Heart*, p. 174, New World Library, Novato, CA., 1999; 6. Thomas Berry, quote from *The Dream of the Earth*, p.2, Sierra Club Books, San Francisco, 1988; 7. Bill Plotkin, *Soulcraft*, p. 1. New World Library, Novato, CA 2003; 8. "Bluebird" poem and the review of *Soulcraft* were printed first in "The Ecozoic Reader", Vol 3, #4 (2003), and Vol. 4, #4 (2007), 9. Richard Rohr, *Falling Upward*, p. 74, Jossey-Bass, 2011; 10 .Don Saliers, *The Soul in Paraphrase*, p.11, Seabury Press, 1980; 11. Fred Craddock, *As One Without Authority,* p. 59, Abingdon Press, respectively.

Cataloging-in Publication Data
Futch, D. Greg
Don't Go Back to Sleep: A Memoir as Meditation

1. D. Greg Futch—memoir 2. Family Life—relationships 3.Spirituality—mediation 4. Nature 5. Rural Life—America

ISBN: 978-1-7352249-3-0
Library of Congress Control Number: 2021909356

Printed in the United States of America   10 9 8 7 6 5 4 3 2 1

Memories Publishing
P. O. Box 82516
Austin, Texas 78708
gfutch@hotmail.com

Cover design from painting by Doris Bickley
Designed by Rebecca Byrd Arthur

TABLE OF CONTENTS

DEDICATION

*This little book is dedicated to two families
who nurtured and shaped me:
the Futchs and the Newbernes.*

*The Futch clan shaped my strength and endurance.
And some of my drive and ambition comes
directly from the Newbernes.*

*Many fine and—like all of us humans—imperfect people,
come from these two families. I am indebted to them,
and have a special love for them all.*

The Breeze at Dawn

The breeze at dawn has secrets to tell you.

Don't go back to sleep.

You must ask for what you really want.

Don't go back to sleep.

People are going back and forth across the doorsill

Where the two worlds touch.

The door is round and open.

Don't go back to sleep.

Jalal al-Din Rumi
Kulliyat-e Shams
Translated by Coleman Barks
from translations

AUTHOR'S NOTE

*T*his work is intended, in the first instance, for family and friends. I believe in passing on experience and reflections to those who are interested, or who might be helped in some way. Family history, in particular, is quite important for later generations. Lessons and insights show up in the most surprising places. In my mid-60s now, I feel the need to record thoughts, feelings, and history more strongly than in the past. Beyond my own circle of friends and family, a few other groups might find this of special interest. Those drawn to the spiritual journey, those worried about the earth and environmental decline, and those who suffer without hope for change. For those who decide to read through this narrative, I appreciate your interest, and I sincerely hope there will be something here of value to you.

Every person has a story to tell. I have read my share of memoirs and biographies. Some are very relevant to my own life. Some are inspirational, some sad and dispiriting. Many readers are like me; they find solace, wisdom, warnings, and total shock in the life narratives of others, (be they prominent, or totally unknown). Each story has something important to say, even something profound. So, here in this writing, I will tell my truth. This is partly a memoir, but it is as much a meditation on life as I have experienced it, and what imports I have gleaned. From my perspective, it is a story of wrestling with the Spirit. It is a faith-journey narrative and a reflection on how the Ultimate Reality interacted with one small person, told from that small person's viewpoint.

A central aspect of my own pilgrimage has been our relationship with nature. This theme will be developed in several of the chapters that follow. Suffice it to say, that for me, the natural world is a manifestation of a Greater Whole, and that humanity's impact on, and treatment of, our earthly home, is a deeply spiritual issue.

Structurally, this work is not of one piece. At some points, the book is more chronological, and driven by narrative. Some chapters are focused on themes or even people. As I developed the work, the subject matter at hand determined for me how to proceed. Beyond the matters of structure and flow, there is the question of tone. I think of tone as partly a consistency of voice. If some part of a written piece sounds too different from another, the reader might question if the same person wrote it. But tone is also an emotional, or "affective" characteristic. Does one passage—or chapter—sound upbeat or joyful? Does the next seem tragic or despairing? There is definitely a variation in tone in some of my chapters. The pieces on music, or my father, for example, have a more celebratory, or grateful tone. Other chapters are more sober, or even melancholy. These differences partly reflect the different voices within any human being. They also simply convey the immense complexity of the human experience. So, I have known joy, ecstasy, depression, fear, and even equanimity. All those energies and viewpoints have some "say" in this meditation.

My prayer is that each reader will relate to something here. And that some inspiration, solace, or sense of communion will be felt. I wish you well in your own journey. Peace be with you.

INTRODUCTION

J have used a translation, by Coleman Barks, of a passage from Jelaluddin Rumi as the epigraph of this book. It is a quote that moved me from the very first time I read it. And though Professor Barks has clearly acknowledged that it is not a literal, but a free-form translation, I feel that it poetically conveys deep spiritual truths. So please, just flip back to this passage and re-read it, the following comments will connect easily to "the breeze at dawn."

Since ancient times, *sleep* has been used as a metaphor for many things. One of the perennial subjects is *death*. Sleep as death, and death as sleep. It has been used so many times, it is hard to pick from among the many examples.

"The sleeping and the dead, how alike they are."
Epic of Gilgamesh (c. 1800 BC)

"Behold, I show you a mystery; we shall not all sleep, but we shall all be changed.... And the dead shall be raised incorruptible."
I Corinthians 15:51-52

"To die, to sleep—To sleep, perchance to dream."
Hamlet, Shakespeare

Death is one of the metaphorical meanings of sleep, but it can also connote dullness, unconsciousness, or lack of awareness. This meaning is used often in psychological or spiritual contexts. One of the most famous examples, comes from Buddhism. After his enlightenment, according to the story, the Buddha was asked by someone if he was a god, or some sort of diving being. He replied, "Remember me as *awakened."* Implying, of course, that before his experience, he had in some sense been asleep.

The Rumi quote, as translated by Coleman Barks, can be interpreted in many ways. The first way is a simple meaning that a person awakening from actual sleep should listen for secrets. Therefore, don't go back to sleep, rather, hear what the breeze is saying. For the purposes of this memoir, I'll be focusing on the symbolic meaning closest to Buddha's comment. Most wisdom traditions call upon the spiritual pilgrim to pay attention, to "seek and ye shall find," to carry on in vigilance, so that eventually, one will find revelation, inspiration, and enlightenment. Then, as Saint Paul says, "Where once we saw through a glass darkly, we can now begin to see Reality with greater clarity." This teaching to strive, to not lose heart, to watch and listen for messages from the Eternal, is a theme that runs through all the wisdom traditions.

Beyond the first phrase to "not go back to sleep," there is the following line: "You must ask for what you really want." This declaration is as important as the first one. And it is a comment that can be misunderstood, or simplistically interpreted. We all know that just asking for something in life does not usually bring about its realization, except in trivial matters. Realize that asking for what "you really want," is just the beginning of a process. If you were to ask for a happy marriage, that would not mean that the appropriate spouse just fell into your lap! Without your own work to find a loving and compatible partner, and without your continuing efforts to grow in the relationship, most likely no happy marriage would materialize. Even if you found a wonderful companion, pain and suffering might darken the relationship; and the circumstances might be completely out of your influence or control.

Still, there is a deeper meaning to this admonition. What is it that you *really* want? The question of what anyone truly wants should lead to soul-searching, contemplation, even difficult inner work. Does you really want happiness, or power, or material abundance? Or maybe popularity, a nurturing community, or wisdom? Of course, someone being able to ask for what they really want usually implies that they have the relative ease and security that only about half the world's population enjoys. But if you are like me, and are among the fortunate ones, then the question remains, and becomes even more important.

Is there any truth to the belief (and some theologies) that God or the Universe will help you get what you need or even what you want? With the provision, of course, that one behaves in some manner compatible and in harmony with the will of God or the laws of the Universe. This worldview or belief system was true in much of the Old Testament writing, (with important exceptions such as the Temple destruction and the Babylonian exile), and with even a counter-theme of inexplicable suffering and meaningless events in life. The Biblical books of Job, and especially Ecclesiastes, question what we in modern times might call the "Prosperity gospel." The question of why bad things happen to good people is a very old one.

There are many levels of asking for what you really want. In my case, by my teenage years, I was already becoming determined to find some ultimate truth, some fundamental meaning in this life. Why so much suffering? Was there a God, or not, and if so, what *kind* of God? For me, my asking became a search for an Ultimate Reality, a pilgrimage to learn about the Un-seen. For a while, I followed both science and religion. After some time, I concluded that spirituality and personal transformation brought more wisdom and insight into what is real, than the objectivist, materialist bias of science. Slowly, science itself became less clearly objectivist and materialist.

Because of my love of and sense of communion with the natural world, the last piece of my journey puzzle came into place. It became clear to me, that only with real changes in human priorities, values, and finally, awareness itself, would there be a more benign and sustainable relationship with Mother Earth. That is what *I really wanted.* Not too much to ask, right?

This little memoir is a meditation on my life's journey as a spiritual pilgrimage. And the second theme, humanity's relationship with the natural world, is inextricably tied to the possibility of spiritually "growing up." I'm convinced that if human beings do not change their ways with regard to Mother Earth, we may not survive at all. So the changing of ways is part of the psychological and spiritual maturing we pray will happen. We must mature into a greater awareness of interdependence, of communion, and to an experience of happiness beyond materialism. Will we be able to do that? I am not certain.

ONE

Tuesday, March 18, 2014

Spring is still a few days away, in the calendar sense. But buds are already on the tips of branches. There is more singing from our winged neighbors: the jay, the mockingbird, the titmouse. The air is changing, and one feels, somehow, the renewal. It's sunny, but not hot. A slight breeze, so a pleasant day as I sit in the park in Austin, Texas.

I was born in May, deep into springtime, in the year 1949. So, on May 9, I will be 65 years "old." I don't really feel 65, maybe about 50! Some kind of blessing this is. And nature and Mother Earth have been part of a greater sense of blessing since childhood. I have so many fond memories of outdoor kid adventures that they tend to blur together. This love of the natural world has never diminished in me. And so, in these early days of the 21st century, I feel both hope and pain when I contemplate our planet. Humanity seems to be more destructive to our natural home than ever before. There is a sense of foreboding, and a despair that human beings feel either overwhelmed or indifferent to the continuing trashing of our world.

At the same time, I have a deeper, more fundamental experience of reality, which colors all of my emotions and thoughts. Simply put, this is a consistent, enduring sense of an ultimate Benevolence in the universe. An all-encompassing and timeless Presence and energy that is neither indifferent nor hostile. This Presence, this ineffable Mystery has been spoken of, written about, contemplated, celebrated, worshiped, and argued about for millennia. But It is ever-fresh and always New to each one who encounters It. New and Old at the same time. (I capitalize this Presence out of respect and awe, not out of fear.)

This persistent sense of "Something Greater" affects my awareness of the Earth in many different ways. One of those ways is that I don't consider the Earth, this reality, this life, as my only and final home. This sentiment can be easily misunderstood, and also easily misrepresented. This feeling of non-finality by no means reduces my love, my wonder, my sense of reverence, with respect to Nature, the Earth, and to the Universe in general. I feel completely at home in this wonderful world of sun and storm; birds and bears; cycles of water and wind, growth and decay, beauty and fearsomeness. At the same time, the intangible, and usually invisible, Reality which is manifested through this physical world, is also, in some deepest way, my home. "The two worlds," some have called it.

Our sentiments, our feelings, our thoughts, are all deeply conditioned: by our families, our culture, and our times. And so it is with me. My own awareness of, and affection for, the natural world, is deeply rooted in my childhood, my parents' own outlooks, and in some form of intangible Communion, which endures through all the vicissitudes of my life. Through time, I've also been deeply moved by the writers who have shown a respect and admiration for Nature similar to my own. Whether it be Thoreau, Emerson, Peter Matthiessen, or Mary Oliver, writers express a wonder and awe many of us feel in our encounters with Nature.

As I write these words in 2014, natural systems, and the Earth itself, seem to be under threat as never before in human history. And much of that threat is coming from us, the very creatures who totally depend on this wonderful world. From climate change; to the extinction of many species; to the maxing out of available water and land; to the changing of ocean chemistry and temperature, the list of circumstances potentially threatening to human life is troubling and long. For those of us who already have grandchildren, the feeling of unease—and even despair— can haunt our daily lives. Will the world our grandkids inherit be more hostile than the world our generation has known? This is a common, very disturbing concern for many now, not just those of the "Baby-boom" cohort.

My grandparents on my mother's side grew up on farmland in deep South Georgia. They *did* not know electric lighting or indoor toilets in their childhoods. They did know the work of milking cows, plowing behind mules, the cultivation and harvesting of corn, tobacco, and cotton. They did know the Great Depression of the 1930s. But they also knew love and community; singing and church going; aid in times of need; and huge Sunday family feasts. Their world was hard in so many ways. But they escaped the worst of privations felt by many others, especially during the Depression. And they always had what they needed to survive. And they both felt, for they sometimes told me, an abiding faith in, and sense of, Something Greater. In this, I share a real faith with my grandparents.

My grandparents struggled for a fulfilled life in a very different age. The same is true of my parents who lived through WWII. The world had become much larger for them, in far-away lands, and events became critical for their own lives. And now, we live in a global consciousness. For me, the crisis of environmental degradation, and the quality of human spiritual maturity are intimately entwined. Spiritual growth should expand awareness and wisdom. Thus, from my perspective, only the continuing "evolution" of individuals and societies—in morality, compassion, and insight—can improve the chances that Mother Earth will remain hospitable for human life.

In my own journey, I see the awesome issue of climate change, and the related issue of sustainability to be challenges of the first magnitude. And they require of humanity an evolution of consciousness and a change of heart which might be beyond our capacity. I choose to believe not.

To the satisfaction of the majority of thoughtful people, science has demonstrated the direct affect human activity has had on soil, water, forests, jungles, and ultimately…apparently…climate itself. We Homo sapiens, as a, "life form," have come to dominate the planet, for good or ill. Our stewardship of the natural world can be viewed economically, politically, biologically, ethically, and even spiritually. In fact, for many of us, the human treatment of Earth's dynamic systems is indeed most fundamentally a spiritual issue. That is, our values, our priorities, our awareness, and wisdom are all reflected in our treatment of Nature. And what we see mirrored back is not comforting.

BLUEBIRD

Saw a bluebird today
 in the Hill Country of Texas

Haven't seen them much,
 rare treat it was

The more experience and time goes by,
 the more I reflect

The more it seems that
 all things have meaning

All things, "good or bad"
 pleasant or not
 clear or obscure

All things have import.

The bluebird was so beautiful,
 it stops your breath,
 if you pause enough
 to absorb it.

What means this sign for me?
 "Nothing," the cynic says

"Who can say?"
 the philosopher replies

but they have no sight
 to feel what is there.

The gift is given
    so still and free

Light and clean,
    so simple, see?

Cling not,
    love life,
    shine bright,

    quiet be.

Nature yields
    these gems
    like rain or shine

Spirit talk
    but not in words.

Eyes to see,
    ears to hear.

Child-like openness
    is dear.

So bluebird flying through the wood
Gave me joy and serene I stood.

Glory lies all about,
    pain and truth,
    love and doubt.

TWO

Early Experiences in Nature

*If the earth does grow inhospitable toward human presence,
it is primarily because we have lost our sense of courtesy
toward the earth and its inhabitants, our sense of gratitude,
our willingness to recognize the sacred character of habitat,
our capacity for the awesome, for the numinous quality
of every earthly reality.*

—Thomas Berry *The Dream of the Earth*

My early childhood was spent in rural south Georgia. The farmland my father grew up on was only about five miles outside the little town of Adel. It was gently rolling countryside with fields and meadows surrounded by pine and hardwoods. A small stream—sometimes in earlier days was big enough to require a ferry—formed one of the boundaries of the Futch property. There were all manner of creatures on this land as I grew up: Rabbits and squirrels, woodpeckers and crows, rattlesnakes and lizards, bobcat and deer, and so many more. Walking this land with my father was a great adventure for me, and I felt most at home and was happiest on these rambling excursions.

There were fields of peanuts, soybeans, tobacco, corn and watermelon. There were pastures of grass for cows, and other lots left in clover to rest the soil and renew the nitrogen. There were woods of oak and pine, and further toward the river, sandy soil and tropical plans such as ferns, and finally, the black lazy winding of the Withlacoochee. Geologically, this part of Georgia is coastal plain, ad was underwater in prehistoric times. The "bottomlands" near the river was left in brush and timber, and was often the site for fishing and hunting.

But there were also ponds on the property, which were used for both irrigation and fishing. We caught bream, perch, and catfish in these reservoirs. Occasionally, there would be a fish fry close by the water. There were happy events where kids either swimming—if in safe water—or created their own adventures in the woods and fields. The natural world and the human world were fully integrated in the experiences of seven and eight-years-olds such as myself, and my relatives and friends. There was contentment and a definite joy.

There is much more I could write about concerning my childhood and the natural world. But most importantly, I want to say that I had a feeling of communion without knowing what the word meant. The feeling of being completely at home when I was out in nature was dominant. This world was where I belonged, and I was as much a part of this world as with any other part "animate" or not.

My father served in the Army Air Corps during World War II. After the war, back in rural Georgia, he must not have been happy with the prospect of living out his life there. This impression comes from the little things he said, and from my experience with him in a general sense. He found a job as a computer programmer—in about 1958 or so—on an Air Force based near Macon, Georgia. Hired as a civilian to work on the base, he was evidently trained there, as he had no experience with computers previously. Those were the early days of programming, I will have a bit more to say about this phase of my. Father's work in the chapters that follow.

One summer, a couple of years after we moved to Macon, my father was given an assignment at the opposite end of the country—in Sacramento, California. I never knew whether he volunteered for the assignment or if he was simply asked to go there, but it didn't matter. My folks, my brother, Ronnie, and I, packed up and prepared ourselves for a road trip across the great U.S.A. We were all excited. We had enough time to visit some of the great western landscape attractions: the Painted Desert, the Petrified Forest, the Grand Canyon, Yosemite Valley, and others as we had the chance.

I still remember, after about 40 years, approaching the Grand Canyon's south rim on the park's winding road. Here and there, the road would come just close enough for a glimpse of the great chasm—its huge open spaces beckoning—a wondrous (mostly hidden) spectacle. The full view awaited our arrival in the parking lot and a quick run to the rim. My brother and I were unable to contain our anticipation. What a magnificent and overwhelming vista! It is beyond adequate description. I just remember I was almost in a trance, trying to absorb the vast distance; the silence; the colors; the tiny string of water at the bottom; the layers of strata; the impression of great age and huge geological forces.

I was in awe and the impact on me was a spiritual one. I remember a childlike thought I had: If a criminal could be brought to see this, then *somehow,* that person would be humbled and changed inside by the majesty and beauty, the implication and wonder, the mystery throughout the universe. Of course, I could not have articulated those words, but I did feel an immature version of those sentiments, which I I'm sure were in my heart.

The feelings of amazement and awe are common reactions to many of nature's spectacles. There is some deep response within us, perhaps, even, some sort of recognition of greater forces of a much larger Reality. It is not simply the grandeur and beauty that resonates with us, the wonders of the natural world have the power to touch us—our best attempts to describe the sensation is in terms of heart and soul. What avails us is the potential for spiritual experience. Nature-based spirituality has been prevalent in indigenous societies throughout time. Many societies have been fully aware of this numinous aspect of the natural world. The truth is, it is the loss of this awareness that characterized technological civilizations. Philosophy and science has contributed to an "objectifying" of nature, and the consequent loss of the sense of the Sacred in that very nature.

At the beginning of his landmark book, *The Dream of the Earth,* Thomas Berry wrote the sentence quoted at the beginningh of this chapter. I would qualify Berrry's remarks in the following way: we are not talking about nature's own upheavals such as earthquakes, volcanoes, and storms. We are talking about human-caused degradation and destruction of our natural environment. The unsustainable dumping of toxins in the air, water, and underground; the removal of topsoil, forests, and wild lands in general; the rapacious, mindless pollution and exhaustion of the resources that are/were part of the gift of Earth to us. Humankind's attempt to become lords over nature, rather than serve as cooperative partners with the billions of years of evolution and experimentation that Earth represents. Humankind's attempts to become lords over nature—rather than serve as cooperative partners with Earth's billions of years of evolution and experimentation—is always stunning.

Humility and some deeper patience will perhaps yet "save" us. Many have concluded that without changes in human awareness and understanding, no amount of technical "fixes" can rescue us from ourselves. The natural world is our home. But our restless grasping and immaturity are trying to break the boundaries of this world. There are limits to resources. There are limits to excess. There is accountability in Reality in general. Humanity now is at risk of paying a very high price for waste and willful disregard for natural systems of balance much more profound than we allow ourselves to imagine.

The scale of issues, such as climate change, oceans becoming more acidic, and the seeming unwillingness of many in power to acknowledge limits to growth and consumption—this reality drives many to despair and resignation.

Are human beings capable of changing our priorities? Is it possible for us to "grow up," and develop a more mature, wise view of human desires and needs? Will evolving consciousness and awareness of the great inter-connectedness of all Reality come in time to save humankind from disaster?

A friend once gave me a copy of Henry David Thoreau's *Walking*. In his typically direct manner, Mr. Thoreau laments the closing in of wild nature. For there is something in the natural world, he says, which draws us on. In regard to which direction to set out when beginning a walk he writes:

> *I believe there is a subtle magnetism in Nature,*
> *which, if we unconsciously yield to it,*
> *will direct us aright. It is not indifferent*
> *to us, which way we walk...* [1]

Thoreau's sentiments and intimations are echoed by many great writers around the world. Even the apostle Paul seems to have felt that the Creation was evidence in some Transcendent Order. Depending upon whose "exegesis" one wishes to follow, or whether one simply interprets for oneself, this passage from the book of Romans, strongly suggests seeing the natural world as an epiphany:

> *For what can be known about God is plain*
> *to them, because God has shown it to them.*
> *Ever since the creation of the world,*
> *His invisible nature, namely His eternal power*
> *and deity, has been clearly perceived in the*
> *things that have been made.* [2]

---

[1] Thoreau, Henry David. Walking, page 8. CreateSpace edition, Sept. 2013.

[2] New Living Translation Romans 1, https://www.bible.com/bible/116/rom.1.nlt

THREE

My Father: First Mentor and Enduring Role Model

Sidney Brinson Futch was born in 1920 into the farm family of Sidney J. Futch, and Virdie Noah Griffis in deep South Georgia. He was the youngest of nine children, with one brother and seven sisters. From stories I heard about the family farm, the fields were filled with cotton, corn, peanuts, and probably tobacco. There were chickens and maybe pigs. A mule, as well as some milk cows, served various needs. A vegetable garden—full of tomatoes and beans, okra and greens—rounded out the picture of hard-working self-sufficiency. But just barely, and not always. Unpredictable weather, plant pests of various kinds, and changing costs and crop revenue assured that their life was full of toil and uncertainty...a much different picture.

On the other hand, there were times of frivolity and fun, swimming in the creeks and ponds, fish-fries, and church socials, hunting the fields and woods for quail and dove. All was not stress and strain, work and weariness. The Futch clan was an extended family around the little towns of Adel, and Hahira. Aunts, uncles, cousins, and in-

My father and his father. Photo taken sometime in the late 1930s on the family farm.

laws made up an actual community of relatives who mainly lived off the land. I have a photo of my dad when he was about 15, standing next to his father. The mid-1930s photo depicts an elder Futch, a bit thin, but looking resolute in work clothes, suspenders, and hat. My dad is only a few inches shorter, with hands in his overalls, barefoot, a slight smile on his face. It is a moving photograph of a father and son standing in front of a farmhouse. The black and white photo captures something of the spirit of both of those men.

The Futch ancestors seem to have come from lands close to the current German-French border. The old country name was apparently Fuchs, according to all the information I was able to gather. Genealogy work on websites, census records, and some published materials have my forbears landing in the Cape Fear River area of present-day North Carolina in the early 1700s. Although there is some record of how my Georgia ancestors acquired the land they lived on, I am not positive. I read something about a grant of land to an ancestor who had served in the American Revolution. I also read remarks about a land lottery. Regardless, by the middle of the 1800s, Futch folks were in Georgia, and there was an extended Futch settlement in what today is Cook County, Georgia.

My father's seven sisters and one brother had names, more or less common in the Southeast United States of that time: Carra, Vennie, Lottie, Wilma, Fleeta, Mae, Myrtle, and Loy. Through snippets about their childhood lives, I concluded that it was a life full of hard work, but with the extended clan looking after each other, and providing a network of support. My dad always communicated his love of the farmland, for it was rich with memories. But I also sensed his love of the natural world in general. When I was little, perhaps five- or six-years-old, Pop *(dad, father or Pop are all the same person in this writing!)* would take me on walks around the farm. Sometimes my brother would come too. My brother, being 18 months younger than me, could not walk far on his own. So, he was soon hoisted up on my father's shoulders. Meanwhile, little Greg learned to keep a steady pace, trying to keep up with my "old" dad. I have genuine

33

D. Gregory Futch

memories of these walks, and they are sweet, comforting, and happy memories.

The seasons, the soil, the growing plants, the behavior of the creatures, the challenges and the blessings of farming the land: all these wonders and many more, were first pointed out to me by my father. As I walked the farmland with Dad, I of course knew nothing of his earlier life, before my brother and me, before our mother. I knew nothing, for example, about WWII, and his part in it. Years later, I learned the riveting story:

My father turned twenty-one years old on the day Pearl Harbor was bombed. Along with thousands of his countrymen (and women), he joined up, and was ultimately accepted into the Army Air Corps (the precursor to the U.S. Air Force). He trained to be a pilot, and was sent to places such as Eagle Pass, Texas, and others, for this preparation. Dad once told me he almost "washed out" in this training, but he made it; and after earning his wings, he was eventually shipped overseas, to England. There are many things I do not know about my dad's WWII experience, because he, like many men of his generation, would not volunteer information, or in any way boast of his circumstances in the war. I do know that the aircraft he was to fly, and the one which proved to be a WWII workhorse, was the P-47, the "Thunderbolt..." nicknamed "The Jug." This plane escorted bombers, ran strafing and bombing missions, and served as an effective fighter craft against the German Luftwaffe.

Sometime in 1943 or 1944, my father shipped out to England, the staging area for missions against German positions on the continent. The tide had been turning against the Third Reich for some time, and by early 1945, planning meetings were already under way for post-war arrangements between Allied powers. But the fighting was far from over. My father was in the air with his squadron in late February of that year, soaring somewhere over the Black Forest in Deutschland. There is an account in Army Air Corps archives of this last sortie that he flew. At some point, Pop's plane began losing oil pressure, and after radioing this information to the leader, he bailed out. It is not clear in what I read whether the P-47 had been hit by enemy fire, or something else caused the problem.

My father climbing into his P-47, circa 1943-1944.

Regardless, he soon was riding his parachute down into the trees of the "Schwarzwald." From this day in February of 1945, my father was listed as "missing in action." His brothers and sisters, and his "girlfriend" (future wife), Ferry, had no way of knowing if he was alive or dead.

I was told that when he finally returned home to South Georgia, he sat down with the extended family and told them his story...once. He made it clear he did not want to repeat it over and over. I learned the following from brief conversations with him:

He landed in the trees and climbed out of his chute and down to the ground. He said he could have stayed in the woods, but thought he might get lost, so he found a road, and followed it. Soon enough, patrolling German soldiers found him and added him to a group of POWs they had collected. Eventually, he wound up at a POW camp, Stalag VIII A, near the town of Moosburg. My dad revealed few details about this ordeal. He and a German soldier got into a brief altercation, a bit of a pushing match, on the way to the camp. Out came the German pistol, and with the gun against his head, my dad had no choice but to become more cooperative. He was not trying to be a martyr, so he restrained his temper from then on, and lived through the detention. A few months later, April 29, 1945, Allied forces came through the area and liberated all the camps. I know little more than that about his WWII experiences.

After the war, Pop went to work for a farm implement and supply business: the Adel Trading Company. Since he was raised on a farm, Dad probably found this job easy to get used to, but he never said much about it.

How my father met my mother, Ferry Newberne, is an essential part of our family lore. Both were born and raised in the same South Georgia area near the small town of Adel. Both were the youngest child born in their respective families. They went to the same high school, but my father was probably a senior when she was a freshman. They knew of each other, my mother once said, but did not have any contact. My Pop volunteered for military service in 1941. This would haveе been only a couple of years after his graduation from high school. When my mother finished high school, she at some point made the decision to enter nursing school in Atlanta.

The most likely scenario of how my folks met is that after some intital period of my father's military training, he returned home to visit family and friends. My mother tells the story that she was in town for some reason, and spied this young man decked out in his Army Air Corps uniform and was impressed. Perhaps they recognized each other. Somehow the conversation began, and this interaction led to dating, and then to letters between them, hers from nursing school, and his from wherever he was posted at the time. My brother and I still have some of these letters.

In August of 1947, my parents were married. The previous March, my mother had graduated from Grady Memorial Hospital's school of nursing in Atlanta. The next year, she was licensed as an R.N. by the state of Georgia, and began her career as a public health nurse in Cook County, GA. Besides working for the Adel Trading Company, Pop also worked for a while with my mother's father in his State Farm insurance agency in Adel. There are vague memoires of my father's restlessness, in terms of work and the sense of vocation.

My mother, Ferry, in her Grady Nursing School outfit, circa 1946. Photo probably taken on Ponce de Leon Avenue in Atlanta.

In 1957, Pop found out about openings for computer programmers at Warner Robbins AFB, not far from Macon, GA. My guess is that this early work was part of an IBM and Air Force collaboration. I was given to understand that the people hired came on as civilians, even though they worked at the base. My dad began work in this new field and though I don't remember much about it, there seemed to be an optimism and energy in him at that time. I believe there was challenge and excitement for him, and in some real ways, this labor embodied the future of technology and culture. I think he saw it that way.

The final step on my father's career path came when he saw an ad in an Atlanta newspaper from an airline offering computer programming jobs. The airline happened to be Delta, and he began the adventure of helping automate Delta's reservation system. My parents seemed to have a confidence that their fortunes were improving, and that exciting times were ahead for all of us. And so they were.

Through many twists and turns in our family life after we moved to Atlanta. Pop kept long hours at the computer center, and the grueling work kept him from coming home until late. My dad was a goal-oriented worker who embraced the challenge. Pop was not a cold or distant father. My brother and I always felt his love and attention and he found ways to spend time with us, from Cub Scouts, to hiking trips on our vacations, to sports events like Georgia Tech football. My memories are of a loving, compassionate presence, but of one who expected us to do our best in school, to exhibit courtesy and respect in our dealings with others, and who modeled those latter traits to us. We loved and respected our dad.

Although there continued to be many happy times in our family life, by my high school years, I began to notice that my mother had problem, which I did not understand. By the time I was a junior in high school, I realized her struggles involved alcohol. Changes of behavior and personality I had noticed earlier now could be seen as related to her drinking. My mother's "demon" showed up enough to throw a shadow of unpredictability and sorrow over our lives. Certain social events seemed to trigger her drinking, (sometimes, parties or backyard gatherings were occasions when she became clearly inebriated). The toll this took on my father became clearer to me over time. If there was an event planned, and my mother wound up being intoxicated, my father's hopes for a relaxing and pleasurable evening were dashed. After several of these incidents, I know he became wary and learned not to necessarily expect a happy time at social events. After many years, during which my mother's drinking continued, he clearly lost hope of her being able to change, and his own demeanor became less jovial and less optimistic.

In spite of this shadow, the first half of my high school years I remember as being times of happiness, challenge, family vacations, personal achievement, and a community of friends. Our family could fly on "stand-by" passes on the airline, and we took some fine trips together during this time. I was fairly popular at school, and I enjoyed camaraderie there and at church, and even at the Boy Scout troop I was in for a couple of years.

One of the dominant impressions I always had of my father was that of integrity. Soft-spoken, he nevertheless made his own ethics and morals clear in his work, and in his life in general. He followed through on commitments and was consistent in his fair and even gentle treatment of others. These qualities were communicated to my brother and me by word and deed. But not by preaching. Pop did not lecture us on rules or manners. He taught by example. For me, he was a model of strength and quiet dignity. He had a good sense of humor and an easy smile and laugh. My father was not perfect, but he was a very fine human being.

Upon my graduation from high school in the spring of 1967, Pop took the whole family on a trip to

My dad swinging me around when I was about one and a half years old, 1951.

Europe. This was a grand adventure for us. My brother and I had our first exposure to the great cities of London, Paris, Rome, and Copenhagen. We spent about three nights in each destination. And while this seems rushed, we made the most of our tight schedule.

In London, we saw the tourist sights of Buckingham Palace, Trafalgar Square, and the Tower of London. We soaked up the atmosphere and every meal was a new experience. Long hair, mod outfits, and British rock and roll were going strong. In Paris, I was able to use some of my high school French when asking the hotel clerk about accommodations. We saw the Mona Lisa at the Louvre, and my parents actually allowed us to go along to the Folies Bergere, with its sumptuous costumes in one act, and much tasteful nudity in the next.

Rome truly inspired me. From the Roman Forum, to St. Peter's, to the Coliseum, the majesty, the antiquity, and the cultural significance of these grand edifices thrilled all the members of the Futch clan. My father was a fine tour guide, who obviously was enjoying the experience. These days on vacation in fascinating European locales were definitely some of the most joyous times for our family. To this day, I feel a great blessing from these adventures, which opened our hearts and our minds and all four of us felt joy.

As I will detail later, both my mother and my brother struggled with psychological, emotional, and, in the case of my mother, alcoholism. But these afflictions did not define them as people, and on voyages like this European trip, there was happiness and fulfillment for all of us. family without incident.

Of course, I will always be grateful for the good times my dad had. But he had his own struggles. He suffered from a terrible physical condition, which began to stalk him in his mid-forties: Rheumatoid arthritis. This scourge was, and still can be for many, a debilitating disease. It may have been that, or the treatment for it, which contributed to his early death. He remained mobile until his passing, but pain and slow movement were his daily experience. He used many of the treatments prescribed in the mid-1980s: Motrin, gold shots, and finally: steroids.

These gave some relief. But he was often up much earlier than his work required just so he could sit in hot water and loosen his joints. The pain and the stress took a yearly toll on him.

The other source of stress and melancholy for my father was his my mother's drinking. As I have noted already, my mother often drank before social occasions, and was clearly inebriated at a variety of gatherings, especially those that happened at our home. I don't know if Pop ever considered divorce because of my mother's alcoholism, but I could tell in his later years that he had given up on seeing her permanently sober.

On the other hand, there were other areas of my father's life that I know brough him peace and fulfillment. We all had good visits to the farm and with the extended family in South Georgia. He still felt a connection with the land where he grew up. Pop was also active in the Methodist church in our suburb of Atlanta and served in various leadership roles there, where he was well respected and admired. Upon his passing, the minister of the church initiated a service award in his name, to be given annually to a man in the church who exemplified service and integrity.

At one point, Pop served as a "loaned executive" from Delta Air Lines to the United Way, where he was recognized for his commitment and fundraising ability by the charity itself. There are many other aspects of my dad's life I could relate here, but I just wanted to give a sense of his character. He was a genuinely thoughtful and compassionate person. He had his own weaknesses and limitations, which to me were small compared to his virtues and strengths.

I have three stories to share about my father, which give a sense of his compassion—even tenderness. The first is an amusing vignette from the Richard Nixon Watergate years. I had never been a fan of Dick Nixon: he seemed a consummate politician, a "Red-baiter," a manipulator of fear and negative emotions to further his own career and agenda. I assumed he probably believed a lot of the law-and-order first and understanding-last philosophy that he preached, but that did not make him any less disgusting to me. Over the years, Pop and I had a calm and courteous discussion about Mr. Nixon. Pop had voted for him, at least once. But his own thoughts and feelings about him were mixed. When the day came that it looked likely he would be impeached and convicted, Nixon resigned from the presidency. The Watergate hearings, the *Washington Post,* and Woodward and Bernstein had turned the tide. At some point, Pop and I were commenting on the turn of events, and he said something like, "Well, Greg, you were right about Nixon".

I was impressed by my Father's willingness to change his views, to look impartially at evidence, and by his wish to acknowledge validity in a position I had held which differed from his own.

Another story comes from the troubled time in my life when all my dreams seemed to be dying—a time I will describe later as "the collapse of Greg." I don't really remember how I broke the news of my girlfriend's pregnancy. I do recall my father's gentle reaction. He did not judge or condemn me. In fact, he was almost sympathetic to my plight. During the course of events, I learned that my own mother had been pregnant at the time that they married. So, there were clearly many reasons why my father was not harsh when he heard the news. But his compassionate manner helped me in bearing the load of my responsibility, and I'll always remember that.

My last story here is about my final visit with Pop before he passed. Sometime in the first half of 1978, I flew home from Austin to visit my folks. We had a good time together, catching up on our lives, and telling stories. My parents were in a relaxed mood, and one day near the end of my visit, my father spoke up with: "So Greg, how are you doing, really, and what do you see in your future?"

I answered honestly: "You know, I'm not sure what lies ahead for me, but I do feel that the Good Lord will guide me in some way." I truly felt that way, just as in many ways, I still do.

My father had a very comforting reply, "Well, that's good enough for me."

It was just a few weeks later when my father suffered an aneurysm in the brain, and after exchanging a few words with Mom, lost consciousness, and soon passed from this world.

At age 57, he was still what we would call a young man. It was a great loss for me, and our family, and his many friends. I will forever be grateful that I was able to visit with Brinson Futch one last time before he was gone. In fact, I consider it a sign of grace that it happened.

My father's impact on me has many dimensions. His compassion and integrity were modeled throughout our lives together, and I came to emulate, as best I could, those qualities. He had a gentle and unassuming manner, and I hope I've come to be more like that myself. He definitely had more of a temper in his younger years. I also, was not afraid to show anger when it seemed appropriate—and perhaps sometimes when it wasn't. I inherited my father's honest love of the natural world. Thanks to him, I always feel at home in nature, and feel that sense of communion I mentioned earlier.

Naturally, there were the areas of life and experience in which I differed from my dad, and he allowed me that—even respected it. One very significant part of my father's life became, for me, something to avoid. I believe that he never knew of my convictions on this subject— that would be the matter of my mother's drinking and his gradual sorrowful acceptance of it as unchanging. I came to view this situation with all its pain and suffering, as one I would definitely not accept. Or, if I found myself in some relationship or life predicament that was similar, I would find some way to alter it, or get out of it altogether.

In most ways, this is a healthy feeling and conviction. But life is much more complex than picking and choosing or staying and exiting. Over time, this reality would become very clear to me. And I believe my father saw this complexity much better than I did as he came to the end of his time on earth. I will always love my dad, and sometimes I still talk to him in spirit, and in prayer.

FOUR

Change and Continuity

Our family moved from small town Adel, Georgia to the large town of Macon when I was midway through the third grade. I remember my feelings of grief from leaving friends, relatives, and familiar places...and the anxiety of starting over. Like most places and times, Macon, GA of the late 1950s was a mixed blessing. Dad was learning computer programming at the Air Force base. Mom was doing her nursing. My brother and I attended to the same school.

The slow-paced Macon was clad with pine-trees and azaleas. The town was both hospitable and provincial. Racism ran just beneath the surface. It was not ugly and up-front, but the perennially accepted notion of, "Just the way it is" persisted.

For Ronnie and I there were many carefree adventures at this time in our lives. We played with neighborhood kids to our heart's content. We put rocks across a near-by stream and splashed around in the pool; we played baseball on an open space close to home, shot arrows from dime-store archery sets, did the hula-hoop craze, and had our dad help us with one of our biggest thrills: homemade go carts. They were made from 2 by 4s with sawed off brooms for steering columns. Baby stroller wheels, and rope wrapped around the broomsticks and down to the front cross-board, allowed us to turn right or left. We had a dirt road hill in front of our house and spent many hours racing other kids with their own go-carts. The urchins of our neighborhood had more fun than anyone, anywhere!

Electronic games were a thing of the future, and most of our play was outdoors. Even before our parents were Cub Scout pack leaders, they took us all on trips to the weather station, and other notable institutions, but we especially liked the annual pinewood derby races, for which we fitted out our own little cars. We were serious about advancing from Bobcat to Wolf to Bear in the scouts.

Of course, it was not all sweetness and light. A couple of the neighborhood kids were rough characters, and two of my childhood fights came against those boys. One fancied himself a tough guy and lived close by. Our tussle ended when my arm around his neck and windpipe stopped him from biting me. The other one was older and bigger than I was, and our confrontation ended in a stalemate. As a child growing up in the South, I had to be prepared to stand up for myself. It was not extreme, but there was definitely a macho climate. These physical conflicts were a very rare occurrence for me, and I don't remember any others.

My brother Ronnie and I were constant companions, and we could always have fun together. He and I both have fond memories of this time of our lives. A highlight was our summer trip out west (described in the chapter "Early Experiences in Nature"). Another highlight was our rolling skating outings at a local rink called Durr's. It was a quarter mile indoor skating venue with wooden flooring and plenty of early rock music played over the PA system; this place was very popular with the elementary and high school kids. Hits of 1958 such as, "All I Have to do is Dream" by the Everly Brothers, "Sweet Little 16" by Chuck Berry, and "Tequila" by the Champs rolled down over us as we rolled ourselves at high speed around and around the track. Everyone had a great time. Ronnie and I were very happy there.

After three and a half years in Macon, the family began preparing for another move because my father's programming training was about to pay off. He told us he'd seen a help wanted ad from Delta Air Lines in Atlanta in the newspaper, to which he quickly replied. Delta was initiating a computerized reservation system. His application was accepted, and the summer after sixth grade, my brother and I experienced the same apprehension and sadness we felt upon leaving Adel. We would have to start all over again!

But the fears were balanced by the anticipation of new adventures in the big capitol of Georgia. I know my parents were full of hope and enthusiasm as they looked ahead to new jobs, people, and possibilities. My mother derived much fulfillment from her nursing career. And I could sometimes sense my father's satisfaction as he took part in the cutting-edge challenge of automating reservations for a major U.S. airline.

The family's move to Atlanta around 1960 opened up new worlds, but also brought many new stresses and conflicts. My brother seemed to have a harder time adapting to the changes than I did. Ronnie has told me more than once that I was like an emotional guardian for him. Being the older brother, I occasionally shielded him from the full force of disappointments and psychological upsets that accompany the ups and downs of childhood. Whether by trying to defend or explain my brother in interactions with others, or just being his friend, my behavior was mostly instinctive. But I know what my brother means when he describes this dynamic.

Our first year in Atlanta, we attended the same school, but in the second year, I was off to high school. To make a long story short, he became friends with a couple of boys who, in the end, turned upon him. Not so in a violent way, but in a manner that led my brother to doubt his own worth and judgment. He felt betrayed. While kids can be wonderfully loving and compassionate, children can also be truly cruel to each other. This incident set off a long journey of emotional struggle for Ronnie, and in the dynamics of our family. Unfortunately, he became the younger son who could never quite measure up to the older brother. My brother lost self-confidence. My mother had silent struggles of her own—a problem with alcohol that was revealed earlier in this memoir.

Life is ephemeral. Not illusory (like a mirage), and definitely not trivial. But it is experienced as passing, sometimes more slowly, sometimes very swiftly. To this day, I remember a conversation I had with my father regarding time, and some of Einstein's theories of relativity. Together, we mused that a young person, for example a ten-year-old, has quite a different experience of time than a person in their fifties. I believe this phenomenon is because for a ten-year-old, each year represents one-tenth of his or her life, but for a fifty-year-old, each year is only one-fiftieth of life. As a person ages, each year of life is smaller slice of that life, giving the impression that time speeds up the older one gets.

Mortality and loss are two of the greatest impact on a person's life. Each of us on earth is forced to confront this ultimate truth about life. The many losses we experience are usually painful. My own losses seem small compared to those losses I see in other people's lives. My childhood was, generally speaking, a positive and happy time. Many children lose their innocence, their trust, their homes, or their hope in myriad ways.

As I reflect on these grade-school years from the vantage point of my mid-60s, the ephemeral nature of human life is very real to me. The Buddha, living some 500 years before Jesus of Nazareth, taught that nothing is permanent in this life, and that clinging to any particular condition, situation, place, or even time, will inevitably lead to suffering. This is one of those classic insights that must be balanced with "common sense," for it can be interpreted to mean that one should not be overly committed to anything in this life. But one need not become indifferent, apathetic, or lacking in care or compassion to understand the basic truth of the Buddha's teaching. It is a matter of perspective and context, and one might say.

Insights and wisdom are often hard-won. The basic paradox of human maturation seems to require suffering and pain in order for us to learn some of the critical truths regarding values, relationships, morals, and priorities. Thus, discomfort and unhappiness are apparent requirements in human growth. Is that a "good" thing, or a "bad" thing?

It is important to know that, in so many ways, I felt good and loved, and had a sense of empowerment at this stage of my life. I had been able to navigate and manipulate the circumstances of my existence in a way that has brought excitement, joy, and indeed, happiness. This is significant, I believe, for its direct relevance to my personal spiritual journey. I believe that if a human being develops a relatively stable ego and some self-esteem, then some part of the spiritual work may come easier. This is not a new proposal, of course. Many have taught that one must have a more-or-less secure ego before one can begin to deconstruct, or see through it, in the spiritual pilgrimage. On the other hand, many folks seem to have weak self-esteem, but in many ways manifest a compassion and strength of spirit which only an authentic humility can produce. I think of "marginal" people here, whether one finds them on the street, or in mental wards, or in other areas of life where society's "winners" don't usually go.

As I've said, life is transitory. We do not sense this when we are young, living so much in the moment as kids. Time and experience bring this awareness. Events, situations, and relationships—all phenomena—are passing. But these phenomena leave an imprint that shapes a person's identity and consciousness. We humans are "channels" for lived realities, but at the same time, are interpreters, meaning-makers, of all that lived-out phenomena.

My parents tended to be moderates in many areas of life: politics, religion, and general worldview. In fact, I remember my dad quoting with approval the ancient saying, "Moderation in all things." In 1950s rural Georgia, they did not express a racial prejudice, which I perceived in many other folks I encountered. Make no mistake: they were not reformers, or Civil Rights advocates per se. They just seemed to have a relaxed and non-condescending perspective on racial relations. As a girl, my mother, for example, played with a little black girl who lived down the road. This relationship might have been looked down upon or even prohibited in some households of that era. And my father seems to have been influenced by many factors, not least by his WWII experience of meeting and mingling with (mostly) men of many classes, races, and backgrounds.

Thus it was that they supported early racial moderates in Georgia—people like Jimmy Carter, and newspaper columnists in the Atlanta papers who expressed views of equality, tolerance, and good will with regard to black-white relations. Eugene Patterson was a well-known editorial writer who won prizes for his very moderate commentary on the racial struggles of that era. My folks even supported a young senator from Massachusetts when he was elected president in 1960. John Kennedy has been written about and spoken about by so many people, I don't believe I could add anything new about him. I just know that he was perceived by my middle-class Methodist Georgia family to be an optimistic, "progressive," exciting, and even charismatic leader. This is a well-known image of JFK, which many people shared at the time.

Kennedy's impact on my family and me is important for a variety of reasons. He seemed to symbolize a youthful, optimistic, forward-looking mentality that was attractive and inspiring. Though his own stance towards Civil Rights was complicated, to say the least, he saw a "liberal" view as politically advantageous. That, and his emphasis on a space program that would land a man on the moon particularly impressed me, as it did many others. Finally, Kennedy's weaknesses, like his womanizing, were not generally known to the public.

And so it was that when the tragic news came in November of 1963 that the president had been assassinated in Dallas, it was like an emotional body-blow. I, for one, was deeply hurt by this terrible turn of events. I felt a certain shadow had descended on my world, and on our country. Little did I know just how many more shadows… and grievings…and trauma lay ahead.

The Buddha's words and wisdom were not in the heart and mind of the 14-year-old boy I was when John Kennedy was killed. Viewing my experiences then, through the lens of a Buddhist perspective, is a later interpretation. What I learned and what I felt as I lived through my childhood and youth is a very complex reality. I know that I learned how to protect myself emotionally. Even though I was the elder of two sons, and had some advantages of "seniority," there was the "price" of being the tougher one, the older one, the protector. This was mostly an unconscious experience.

Still, I learned to damp down the feelings of unfairness, injustice, or vulnerability that came in the course of my life. One learns to protect the vulnerable parts of one's self just as one learns to protect a younger sibling. This seems to be a normal part of the maturing process. And some of these dynamics could be discussed with our parents. But many conflicts and injustices seen in the world were not brought home to the dinner table, or the bedside, for an airing out.

Many names have been given to the inner parts (or voices) of us, which speak up, or hide out at different times: the inner child, the critic, the parent, the "loyal soldier." I developed a good "loyal soldier" to protect the more vulnerable parts of myself. And in the somewhat racist and provincial towns and places where I grew up, I had to take the bad with the good. There were many fine people in my world. But there were forces of fear and ignorance and prejudice that led to many ugly scenes in our country, not just the South.

Many will say this is the struggle that the great majority go through to become a mature and somewhat whole person. This is mostly true, I believe. But each person's story is unique. As I encountered potential conflict in my youth, I learned not to show fear. This can be considered a very adaptive, even healthy response to danger. It also takes a toll inside.

In spite of that, by my sophomore year of high school, in a suburb of Atlanta, I was a fairly healthy and confident teenager. And like my folks, in the life of JFK, as in the life of Martin Luther King, and of others too numerous to name, I saw the hope and the possibility of a more just, more humane world. Therefore, the killings of the Kennedy brothers and King seemed to be victories for the forces of prejudice and hatred. These events, much like the Cuban Missile Crisis I remember well, left me and many others with a feeling that chaos and dark forces of fear and ignorance were not truly under any one's control. I felt a powerlessness that was both frightening, and melancholy.

It left teenagers like myself doubting the ability or the power of leaders, and even just adults in general, to manage the destructive impulses in human nature. So whether it was not showing fear to a bully in school, or not going along with racist conversations or actions, or braving the larger forces of society's conflicts, I came to build an inner shield and an outer persona. Just living in the world brought these challenges to the fore.

So later in life, the wisdom of the Buddha's teaching seemed clear. One suffered less if there was less attachment to an expectation that didn't materialize, and also if one stopped running from situations or people that needed to be addressed. But the very intellectual nature of the Buddhist teaching requires some experience, and some abstraction from that experience. A child, by definition, is not "there" yet. And in children, the heart and the emotions are not as protected as they are later. Part of the wonder of childhood is this innocence—and also one of the great risks.

Jesus had said, "Let the children come to me, do not hinder them; for to such belongs the kingdom of God" (Mark 10:14). I see this wisdom reflecting the openness and trusting nature of children, qualities critical on the spiritual journey. Still, whatever all the reasons may be, I have felt deeply the conflicts and the pains of this life. I felt the fears and the hopes, the joys, and the sorrows. Even as a child.

As the tide rolls in and out, our lives also often alternate between joys and sorrows. Kennedy's assassination at the end of 1963 brought sadness and a certain loss of faith. But just a few months later, in early 1964, a joyous, infectious brand of British rock and roll was about to invade the U.S. airwaves. And my brother and I joined millions of others in thrilling to the sounds of Beatlemania!

FIVE

Music

*Music oft hath such a charm. To make bad good,
and good provoke to harm*
—Shakespeare, *Measure for Measure*

M usic has had an incomparable influence on me
throughout my journey. Music is a unique "language,"
defined and communicated on a nonverbal, universal basis.

I don't remember what music first entered my
childhood experience, but I do remember how my mother
would sing little ditties at bedtime, or at waking time. My
folks both sang hymns at Sunday church services, and both
our radio and television were full of music. Music was not
only part of our culture; it was part of the extended family
I was raised in. My mother's parents loved gospel singing,
and they often included singing at family gatherings at
their home. Beyond that, my mother and her three siblings
formed a singing group headed by their mother on the
piano, and their father as lead. During the 1940s, the
family group sang at weddings and funerals throughout
South Georgia's landscape of small towns and farms.

This regimen produced a certain discipline, and a fundamental knowledge of music, at least at the non-professional level. My Uncle James went on to help form a group at Auburn University that played the "big band" music of that era. My mother, with her beautiful soprano voice, continued to sing in church and at special events. Music was all around me, so it is easy to see how my own love of music came naturally. I had a feel for it, and never tired of melody and rhythm, and the emotional power of great compositions. Early memories of popular music were of Perry Como and Rosemary Clooney, Frank Sinatra and Tennessee Ernie Ford, Harry Belafonte and Patsy Cline.

"Experts" of various kinds say that music reaches deep levels of the human psyche. I also believe that it moves our emotions in ways that are only barely conscious to us. In every age and place, there are conventions, styles, trends, and special masters and musicians. Music both reflects the times we live in, and in many ways, it influences and shapes those very times. I know little of the great music traditions of India, China, Africa, or Latin American. My limited awareness and knowledge is of what I think of as "Western music," starting with the "classical" era of 18th and 19th century Europe and through 20th century popular genres.

Regardless of the culture, time or format, I do know that music has a power to reach deep inside people who might otherwise be mentally disabled, or suffer from dementia, or other memory-impairing ailments. Many stories exist of people who no longer communicate, or recognize those around them, returning to some "normality" upon hearing familiar music. As if coming out of a coma, they might hum or sing along, or even play the piano. And then, when the music stops, they often revert completely to their former condition.

Awareness, consciousness, emotional conditions, "the "soul," for most—if not all of us—are concepts, which are often deeply mysterious. Thankfully, music reaches the spiritual level of our human experience. Along with the aesthetic and emotional impact of music, there is a spiritual "response." Something in the total work of the composition "speaks" to the deep and intangible dimensions of our being, resulting in some sort of non-verbal connection, or communion. The interaction between the music and the listener is sacred. Some aspect of our being responds as we do in only a few other areas of experience, often manifesting in an inner—and sometimes outer—dance.

I believe that sound organized as music reaches a depth within the mind and heart that is similar to the depth touched by the sense of smell. Scent is, by all accounts, among the most potent of the senses, in that it may spark feeling and memory. This appears to be true of music, as well—especially for those who deeply appreciate it.

Music contributed to one of the simple pleasures of my high school years: the large youth choir I was part of at our Methodist church. Approximately 30 or 40 kids sang at Sunday services off and on, but we also toured, singing at various churches throughout the Southeast. Our director was a driven music man, and we worked hard for him. Frequently—but not always—we sounded quite respectable! Our summer tours also included skits, folk and soft rock, and innocent co-ed camaraderie on the tour bus. I have fond memories of this musical and social journey from my youth.

In January of 1964, the Beatles huge hit, "I Want to Hold Your Hand" was being played on American radios. By February, it was the #1 song on the Billboard chart—it held that position for seven weeks. I actually remember where I was when I first heard that song, which was a sound of power and energy and joy to my ears. My formative teenage years were shaped by Beatles' music. As I noted before, music tends to reflect the times it lives in, but it also tends to influence and shape those times. My parents were shaped by the Big Band music of Tommy Dorsey, Glenn Miller, and Benny Goodman. But my most critical years of puberty, late teens and early twenties, were shaped by the pop and rock music of the 1960s.

In the late 1950s some of the big hits were "Bye, Bye Love" (Everly Brothers), "Young Love (Sonny James), and "All Shook Up (Elvis Presley). In the early 1960s pop music was still relatively innocent. Top pop singles in 1962 included "Big Girls Don't Cry" (The Four Seasons), "Loco Motion" (Little Eva), "Duke of Earl" (Gene Chandler), and Chubby Checker's big hit, "The Twist." No anger in these tunes. No political commentary, or even "hard rock" music. But the evolution of pop music from softer, and less intense lyrics and instrumentation was already somewhat evident.

Artists like Elvis Presley, the Everly Brothers, and Ray Charles would all have long runs in pop culture. But just as the folk music of early 1960s USA birthed a harder, more political version later in the decade (especially with Bob Dylan), the whole course of popular music came to reflect the conflicts and tensions of American society.

Still, in 1965, the bestselling album was the soundtrack from the movie Mary Poppins. Top singles included

"Wooly Bully" (Sam the Sham and the Pharaohs), "You Were on My Mind" (We Five), and "Downtown" (Petula Clark). Change was coming with the arrival of the "British Invasion." The Beatles had appeared on *The Ed Sullivan Show* the previous year. The Rolling Stones made their first American tour in 1964, and in 1965, the Stones, the Beatles, and Herman's Hermits (as well as Petula mentioned above) all had top 10 hits on American radios.

So in 1965, when we learned the Beatles would include Atlanta on their American tour, we grabbed up tickets as fast as we could. By that time, John, Paul, George, and Ringo had already released several albums, up to and including the soundtrack to the movie *Help*. In August of that year, with cousins in tow, we all packed into the old Atlanta Braves baseball stadium and joined the fidgety, noisy crowd as we awaited our musical heroes. The Liverpool lads did not disappoint.

Rocking through hits like "Twist and Shout," "Can't Buy Me Love," "Ticket to Ride," and of course, "Help," the boys maintained a very high energy level. And so did we! Mostly yelling, screaming, and dancing to the beat, we were filled with a kind of ecstasy. Joy and harmony, shaking bodies, instant community: that was a Beatles concert in the early 1960s. It definitely goes down as one of my most happy and satisfying musical experiences. The memory is still strong 50 years later! As a youth, I was privileged to see and hear many other great musical artists from many genres. While some matched the intensity of my experience of the Beatles, none of those concerts ever gave me a more joyful, more thrilling, or more complete experience.

Music, for me, is a gift from God. It is one of the blessings of human existence. And I will always be most grateful. I could give a detailed account of every song, artist, and concert that has impacted me over the years, but instead, I will offer a reflection on this excellent dimension of our cultural reality. I use the word "cultural" with deliberation because music and the times are inextricably interwoven. As I have already mentioned, the decade of the 1960s and its music, is, for me, a particularly significant example of this truth. The energy and the conflict flowing from the Civil Rights movement, Vietnam, the counterculture, and political turmoil, fueled much of the musical art of this time. It was thrilling, and comforting, and reflected anger, and sadness, and hope, and all the other emotions of that crazy era. There was a generational "push" to find better ways of living, more honest and less restricted by the habits of the past.

The music reflected all that. Rock, soul, jazz, and blues all became more creative, more inspired by the times, more overlapping with the other genres. Of course, I was heavily influenced by all that, being a great lover of music to begin with. Many different kinds of music touched me. I could be as moved by Dionne Warwick singing a Burt Bacharach piece as I was by a fine performance of Mozart or Tchaikovsky. Blues and R&B were great loves of mine. I tended to listen to Ray Charles and John Lee Hooker, but a solid groove, or a great melody were equally important. James Brown was a favorite: no one funkier! In my lighter or more reflective moments, Simon and Garfunkel, or some of the folk greats were my choices.

But there were a few artists and bands of my generation who stood above the others. For me, those brighter lights included the Beatles, and the Rolling Stones, Neil Young and Eric Clapton, the Allman Brothers and Led Zeppelin. Others too numerous to list gave me endless hours of entertainment. However, besides the Beatles, two other artists stood at the top of this musical pyramid: Bob Dylan and Jimi Hendrix. These two in particular defined rock and roll excellence for me.

Dylan was the poet and songwriter for my generation, but he also clearly loved a great rock and roll groove to match and support the lyrics. And Hendrix became the master of the sonic potential of the electric guitar; he was my favorite musician on that instrument. Dylan and Hendrix, in different ways, were innovators and creators of a special kind. The poetry of Dylan's songs opened the hearts and minds of listeners who felt something of their own experience in the lyrics. Hendrix gave expression to an emotional, even psychic reality within the listener's being. They both were political, and their critiques and commentary were very powerful. But it was the combination of the song and the lyrics that worked the magic, regardless of the subject matter. You could say that in Dylan, the music supported the words of the song, whereas in Hendrix, the reverse was true. That is, the lyrics were poetry in Dylan, but with Hendrix, the sound of the music was dominant. The creativity and the power of the music of this era gave me—like so many others—hope and inspiration. And so, as sort of a sequel to my Beatles' concert story, I have to say something about seeing and hearing Jimi Hendrix.

In the very turbulent year of 1968, Jimi Hendrix came to Atlanta. He played two shows in August at the old Atlanta Metro Auditorium. I remember it was used for pro wrestling matches, and other events. Vanilla Fudge opened for the Experience. In 1968, "Are You Experienced" was the top-selling album of the year. Jimi and company had taken the country by storm after appearing at the Monterey Pop Festival the year before. And I had been a fan since I first heard "Hey Joe" and "Purple Haze." So on the day we went to hear him, I was definitely pumped up.

After the opening act, the curtains remained closed for a while, and there was quiet from the stage. The audience was restless and impatient to hear the guitar phenomenon. Finally, there was the soaring sound of guitar chords and notes, with that distinctive bending, distortion, and "soulfulness," which was so characteristic of Hendrix. This tune-up brought the crowd to its feet, and there we stood for most of the concert, as I recall. The audience screamed and cheered, and was completely awed by the spectacle and this sound like no other. I actually don't remember the songs the Experience played, but a set list posted on line from that concert included "Red House," "Wild Thing," and "Purple Haze."

The power and the innovation and the mastery of the instrument were all on display during this concert. I was transported and ecstatic to be seeing what I knew, even then, was a truly unique and unprecedented talent. I feel a definite blessing in having seen and heard Jimi Hendrix. Many have tried to put into words his artistry. The most critical point for me was that I felt the heart and soul of the musician was being expressed. The emotions and the psychic energies were fully engaged, if the listener allowed it. Hendrix was at one with his instrument, and we all *felt* the depths, the colors, and the energy of the melody and the lyrics. The music came ALIVE.

Hendrix was a shooting star. There was a lot of sadness in his life, starting with his childhood. He knew pain in relationships; he knew the highs and lows of a back-up and session musician. But he also knew the heights of musical creativity and of transfixing an audience. He apparently was a shy man by nature, and his music was his way of interacting with the world. A sense of humor and a yearning for a better world were evident in his actions and in his lyrics.

That was August 1968. By 1969, he was a worldwide star, and closed the Woodstock festival with that awesome rendition of the "Star Spangled Banner." I was a huge fan of Jimi Hendrix, and thus it came as another stunning blow to my psyche when in September of 1970, he was found dead in bed in London. At 27 years of age, this musical avatar had passed from our world.

I will always be moved by the music of Mozart, Beethoven, and Bach. I am literally lifted up inside when I hear great gospel singing, or Mahalia Jackson, or Louis Armstrong. And I share many of the musical joys of my parents' generation: Duke Ellington, Frank Sinatra, and the big bands of the 1940s. But my own life's soundtrack, as I've said, was the music of the late 1950s, 60s, and the early 70s. So, although I will continue to appreciate great fine music of later generations, my coming of age was accompanied by the Everly Brothers, Elvis Presley, the Beach Boys, the Four Tops, B. B. King, the Supremes, Marvin Gaye, James Brown, Ray Charles, Simon and Garfunkel, Peter, Paul, and Mary, the Animals, Jefferson Airplane, Crosby, Stills and Nash, the Byrds, the Grateful Dead, Jackson Browne, the Allman Brothers, Led Zeppelin, the Doors, the Mamas and the Papas, Otis Redding, Janis Joplin, the Rolling Stones, Neil Young, and Santana.

And at the top of my list, as I already declared, stand the Beatles and Bob Dylan and Jimi Hendrix. These three were like "forces of nature," and shaped their times—

as much as they were shaped by them. So to my old friend Jimi, I'll just paraphrase his "Voodoo Child" line back to him: *"Since I won't see you again in this world, I'll meet you in the next one. Don't YOU be late!"*

Margaret and me on our 25th Wedding Anniversary, 1997.

Photo taken by Patrick Roques, Margaret's brother.

**Reunion of my mother's siblings (from left):
Uncle James, Aunt Dorothy, me, my mother, Ferry,
and Uncle Paul, circa late 1990s.**

Photo taken by unknown Newberne family member.

Beautiful wedding of Dominic and Beth with their son, Aden at a San Luis Obispo winery, October, 2006. What a wonderful day of joy.

Photo provided courtesy of Dominic and Beth.

Congregational church retreat with me, Bill Beardall, and Dr. Mathis Blackstock

Photo taken by Pat Oakes, member of Congregational Church of Austin.

SIX

Science, Personal Trauma, Disillusion

In the fall of 1967, I began my college experience at Georgia Institute of Technology, in Atlanta. My dreams were not small! I was shooting for an Aerospace Engineering degree, followed by trying to find a job in the U.S. space program. I was inspired by NASA, by Kennedy's charge to put a man on the moon, by science fiction, and by a respect for, and attraction to, the scientific worldview.

Project Mercury had already successfully launched John Glenn into earth orbit in 1962. The Soviets were in a "space-race" with the U.S., and NASA was working hard to get that first human on lunar soil before the end of the decade. It is difficult now to convey the heady atmosphere of excitement, the emotional pull of exploration, and the sense of shared purpose which the space program engendered. Especially for many boys and men of my generation, there was a fine romantic thrill, and a vicarious experience of danger in the triumphs and the setbacks of the early space flights. These adventures fired the imagination of young people like me. In sci-fi stories and films, and in the somewhat dorky TV show, "Star Trek", one could find portrayed the potential glory and possible terrors of humanity's reach into "outer space".

Beyond space exploration itself, was the promise and power of the scientific worldview. My father and I, in particular, shared a lay person's interest in, and focus on, scientific discoveries, and what might be called the "philosophy of science". At least for a teen-ager moving into his 20s, the method of observation, of experimentation, of reproducible results, of skepticism toward superstitious or untested hypotheses.... all this was attractive and "dependable". This approach to reality gave a sense of certainty and, even better, the feeling of understanding the mysteries of nature and the universe. I could have the emotional and psychological impression of "signing on" to the great enterprise of exploration and learning by entering the engineering program at GA Tech in Atlanta. Hope and anticipation were strong elements in my consciousness at this time.

It is important for me to offer some larger context here. I've briefly mentioned MLK and the Civil Rights movement in an earlier chapter. This momentous struggle was transpiring at the same time as I was trying to figure out my own future. The sin of American's slavery history and continuing racism against African Americans was clear to me. But I was still imbedded in a white middle class world which, while sometimes acknowledging this terrible reality, did not give it much deep thought.

The other huge societal struggle at this time was the widening divisions over the Viet Nam war. This was leading to multiple crises in the conscience and culture of our country. And for me, it threatened to become personal. My own feelings about our "domino-theory" war had become more and more troubled. It appeared to me that the conflict in that Asian country was as much a civil war, and a fight against occupying powers –the French first, and then the Americans—as it was an attempted Communist takeover by Russian or Chinese forces.

I respected and admired the bravery and the beliefs of patriotism which led so many young men (and women) to sign up and join U.S. forces in Viet Nam. But when the draft lottery began while I was attending college, it happened that my number was too high, so I was not "chosen." I was relieved, of course, since I had zero desire to go fight in a war which could see both LBJ, and then Nixon, stayed in for political reasons, as much as any idea of a righteous crusade.

Yes, the Civil Rights struggle, and the anti-war movement were both very engaging for me, and deeply affected my worldview. And I did very small things to register where I stood. But I was not intimately impacted— in my own life and circumstances—and for better or worse, these necessary and noble struggles did not lead to any direct involvement from me. The heroes (and heroines) of these major American movements, however, will always be MY heroes and heroines.

So, my passions and commitments to science and the space program led me in that direction, but they did not cause me to ignore the conflicts tearing at the social fabric of our country. And there were other conflicts closer to home, which shadowed the future for me. My mother's developing problem with alcohol stood out, especially before I left home for college. What had started out as social drinking in young adult years, was gradually becoming a dependency. I'll never know all the factors which contributed to my mother's addiction, but I can speculate on a few. Ferry Futch was a child of her generation, and of her culture. Born southern and female, she responded to the conditioning of her time by becoming the charming and socially aware southern lady. Her instincts were to create and sustain harmonious relations in gatherings, in work and family interactions, at church, and in any context where people needed or wanted to be in the company of others. This required a suppression of her own feelings of frustration, anger, and even sadness. When she drank, the repressed "shadow-side" of her being was allowed to come into the light.

There is a vast literature on alcoholism and the children of alcoholics. In perusing some of this writing, I can see some of myself in it, but there is much about my life—I would say most—that doesn't fit into any familial or psychological stereotype. On one hand, many children of alcoholics strive to "fix" or rescue situations or people and lean toward a "care-taking" style of life. This was often the result of trying to cope with the obviously unreliable parent. I definitely have shown some of this behavior. On the other hand, in my case, my mother's drinking only became a problem in my high school years. Most of my childhood, I only knew a normal and loving mother. So in my own long journey, I have tried to let go of some of the "rescuer" tendencies, and just become more self-aware in general. And to repeat, I was blessed during some critical childhood years to have both a healthy and nurturing mother, and a loving father.

It is always difficult, I believe, to reconstruct the past. For my purpose here, I'm striving to say something about my attraction to the scientific worldview, but also about the manner in which my mother had become more "un-dependable." There is, I suggest, a relationship here beyond the other reasons for my interest in science and space exploration. Not only was I growing up, "differentiating", and finding my own way. Beyond the "normal" process by which children learn their parents are not perfect, there was the clear breakdown of my mother's "motherly-ness" when she drank.

So science and the scientific worldview was a very promising foundation for reliability, obvious benefits in real life, and the search for "truth". I'm sure most of this outlook and feeling was only semi-conscious to me. Mostly I felt I could be part of the grand enterprise of expanding knowledge and exploring the mysteries of the universe. Clearly, I was idealistic. I wasn't just looking for a good paying job as an engineer. I wanted to part of the progress of civilization, especially the U.S. part of it!

Wisdom is often hard-won, isn't it? Thus, for example, after a year in school, though I could do the work at Ga. Tech, there was a growing awareness that I didn't really want to be an engineer! If I could have found a way to join the space program with some other kind of degree, I might have pursued it. But my contemplation of working in the science and technology field was becoming less and less attractive. I still believed in the promise and the power of the scientific worldview. But other voices inside me were calling. Looking back at this time, I know that I had always been as interested in pycho-dynamics as I was in aero-dynamics! It seemed to me that no matter how much change happened in the outside world—technology, exploration, manipulation of the environment—if human nature did not change, then all the traumas I had already seen in my short life were just signs of more to come.

And my life was about to change in ways I could not have expected or wanted. After my first full year at Georgia Tech, I contracted mononucleosis in the summer of 1968. Thus began what I have come to think of as the "collapse of Greg"! One thing after another led to the crashing of my ideas, my visions, and my self-image.

The physical illness prevented me from being active. I tried to work and could not. I was exhausted almost all the time. I had never encountered a sickness which so disabled me. When I was a child, I had mumps, and measles. I had faint memories of these. But "mono" truly laid me low. And I was actually flat on my back, resting and sleeping much of the summer of 1968. It was depressing and dispiriting. But there was something else—just as intense, and even more overwhelming—I found that my girlfriend was pregnant!

Without becoming inappropriately personal and intimate, it is important to declare certain realities and dynamics here. So far as I can remember, I never had an honest "sex-talk" with my parents. I believe there might have been some very brief comments from my father. But my own experience seemed to be that of many others of our age and time. Our parents were not very comfortable in talking openly about sex. This most potent and primal force of nature seemed taboo, even shameful, in the minds and hearts of so many people. It was if sexuality was too explosive, too untamable to be discussed in any but the most shallow and superficial manner.

Needless to say, I was lost. Pregnant girlfriend, mononucleosis, and a fading idea of my own vocational future: these emotional and psychic blows left me depressed and despairing.

At some point during that summer, my grandparents came to visit. I was living with my parents during my time of illness. I don't believe I had told them yet about the pregnancy. One evening, my grandmother—who I was quite fond of— came into my room, where I was lying in bed in an exhausted state. Few details of the interaction remain in my memory. But I know she read something from the Bible, a psalm as I recall. Sometime during, or just after my grandmother's visit, I had what I can only inadequately describe as a vision. It was an experience of light and bliss. There were not words, and there was no appearance of any figures—divine or otherwise. But it was a transforming and deeply consoling event for me. I felt a deep and wonderful sense of being loved. And the light was more real than natural light. It was overwhelming.

There were not commands, no directions given, no advice. The nature of the phenomenon, I believe, cannot be truly pinned down. Like many "mystical," transpersonal, or spiritual experiences, its cause, its authenticity, and its meaning, lies in the mind and heart of the one who goes through it. Likewise, those who hear of this event must decide for themselves these questions. I only know that the "incident" left me with a feeling, an awareness, and a conviction, of having been touched by something Real in an ultimate sense.

This "peak experience", so precious to me that I do not like to belabor it here, was not to result in a life less painful, less confused, or less troubled. That is, suffering continued, and still continues. But my inner orientation toward suffering was altered in ways that, to repeat myself, are quite difficult to articulate. This moment in my journey will continue to play a very important role in my narrative.

It is a milestone, and a sign for me. The spiritual and psychic implications echo down through my years and to the present day.

I don't believe that faith in Something Greater has to depend on or require unusual or exceptional experiences. I DO feel that these experiences are often times and spaces of grace, however one chooses to define that term. So, at a time of tremendous confusion, despair, guilt, and self-doubt, I was subjected to a wondrous and inexplicable event. This would not be the last occasion for a major opening of the heart and a significant shift in consciousness.

Some of the psychological and emotional "events" or incidents in our lives are so profound, they tend to transcend even the story we tell about them. I believe my experience of light and bliss was just such an event. But it is critical for me to say that I see this moment of grace as part of a journey, a process, even, perhaps, an unfolding. With great humility, I feel that the opening of mind and heart is an evolution, or a transforming, if you like. I am not very good at it. I just sense that the "Higher Power" never stops reaching out. It's both personal and impersonal. It is like a mother nurturing her child, and at the same time, it is like the force of gravity: Inevitable.

VOICES

Inside me, the perpetual dialogue,
    and often the same argument:

The dark ones smile as
    they talk pain and despair,

it's all futile; the struggle,
    the hope, the sliver of light——

But what are these other voices
    reminding, remembering, whispering?

Some feeling is tied to each,
    a familiar knowing comes forth.

So even when I'm barely
    holding on, keeping panic at bay,

the weariness soaking through,
    there is still this sense,

this illogical, inexplicable awareness
    of being held, of Presence,

of light, of silence, of
    connection returning,

stubbornly remaining, doubting
    the doubt, answering without words,

WHO is THAT?

SEVEN

Later Experiences in Nature

As I've often mentioned, the natural world feels like home to me. In this chapter I'll describe three times and places in which Nature touched me in profound and magical ways.

The first one is comical in many ways. When it happened, I did not label it with any dominant feeling. There were emotions that I felt, but they were varied and no single one colored the event. Over time, the memory has been dominated by humor. I believe all human emotions are reflections of a divine capacity, so, based on my experience, God has a sense of humor!

Some years after my father's passing, when I was still in my thirties, I decided to visit the South Georgia our farmland on my own. Driving down from Atlanta usually took a little more than three hours. It was the type of trip so familiar to me that my mind would wander as I drove. Memories of childhood farm adventures, and ideas of our future stewardship of the land, were part of my reverie. After visiting relatives in town and in the country, I decided to drive out to the Futch property, pitch a tent, and spend the night. I appreciate solitude, and have always liked being outside, so I expected a time of nature sounds and serene reflection. And my stay did have those gifts, but the night and morning had a couple of surprises.

I pitched my tent on the border between a stand of hardwood, and an open pasture. It was a restful time and place, with clear skies, and a comfortable temperature. Crickets, slight breezes in the trees, and bullfrogs in a nearby swamp were the main sounds I heard. I was very much at ease. And soon I was asleep.

Before long, I was awake again. I heard a dog barking off in the distance. Since I was a few miles from any house, I thought the barking would soon stop. Instead, the barking started sounding closer. Oh no, I thought, that hound is gonna come right on over to this tent. And sure enough, I soon heard the loping run, and the dog coming close. The mutt—what else would it be, I concluded—stopped just outside my tent and began to growl!

"For Pete's sake", I muttered, (actually it was something more crude). I pondered how to get rid of this canine. So, my plan was to clap my hands, and at the same time, yell as loud as I could. And without warning, that's what I did. The dog bolted! Racing away as fast as it could, the hound howled back at being so rudely insulted. I was glad the trick worked, and slept peacefully the rest of the night.

Morning was beautiful: soft sunshine with few clouds. Little birds and unseen critters made small noises in the brush. I climbed out of the tent, and, to wake up, sat beside a tree with my back against the trunk. Not many moments passed when I heard a faint rustling sound. It seemed to come from some distance away. But it also seemed to be coming closer. (Where had I seen this movie before?) The sound was of something moving swiftly through the leaves and pine needles on the ground. Before I could even guess what this might be, and while I still leaned against the tree, the mystery was revealed. A beautiful black snake came to an abrupt halt right beside me. It turned its head and was extremely surprised to see me! This creature that moved quickly over the ground was evidently on its morning hunt. The adrenaline rush lifted me right up to a standing position, as the snake shot off through the ground cover at a speed I didn't think possible. Needless to say, it would be difficult to determine which one of us was more astonished and dumbfounded, but even as it happened, I could feel a bit of the comedy of the encounter. This creature, I believe, was a coach whip, or what locals called a "black racer," because it is known for its speed. Completely harmless and striking in appearance, it represented for me an unsentimental experience of wildness.

In later reflection, I considered that in some way, perhaps out of a sense of humor, the Universe had reversed my encounter with the dog in the night. This time, I was on the receiving end of a startling and even shocking visit. I came to view the two events as two acts of a truly comical play.

The next story occurred when I was in my fifties and it requires a bit of setting the stage. After my wife and I returned to Austin in 1994, I eventually found a church I liked, which was Trinity United Methodist, a theologically and politically liberal congregation. I was active in various ministries there, including the cold weather shelter, and ecumenical endeavors. But I particularly was blessed by the opportunity to lead small classes and groups. This had felt like a calling of mine since seminary days. I led classes on theology and spirituality, church history and John Wesley. I enjoyed very much being able to share some of my theological education and, in return, have communion with fellow travelers on the spiritual path.

My own journey was continuing apace. At some point, I asked my minister for the names of potential spiritual mentors. Graciously, he suggested three. All seemed to be fine and worthy people, but one came from a nature-based spirituality background, and that one was Dr. William Taegel. "Will," as I call him, had been ordained as a Methodist minister, but he had a strong exposure to, and feeling for, Native American spirituality. I could spend many pages describing the work of Will and his wife, Judith Yost. But I will confine myself to some of the aspects of their work most relevant to my own journey. Will and Judith had been working with forms of spiritual community for many years. When I met them, their primary focus was the Earthtribe: a nature-based spirituality community. This community practiced some of the rituals of the Lakota and other North American tribes. So, they conducted sweat lodges, and once-a-year vision quests, tailored to a primarily Caucasian and usually middle-class following.

Will and Judith are always very careful and disciplined in carrying out these rituals. Will received extensive training from Native American practitioners, and much preparation went into all the events. I found the sweat lodges to be therapeutic and an experience of community in which chants, prayers, and singing created a healing "atmosphere." These were not warrior sweats.

I saw Will as a mentor and counselor, on a one-on-one basis, for a year or two, and during that time, attended a couple of vision quest encampments. These were usually held on private land, or sometimes on public land that could be reserved with permission. These camps were the "home base" from which individual "questers" spent one, two, or three nights out alone in nature, having fasted and prepared themselves for the experience.

The goal is for one to have some encounter with one's deeper self, with the forces of nature, or, perhaps, with the ultimate Reality which speaks through both the outer and the inner worlds. Thus, one cries out for "a vision:" perhaps of one's calling; perhaps for strength for life's major challenges; perhaps for a deep spiritual insight, if one is able to receive it. After some time in this community, I felt ready for the quest myself. There are many details of this experience I will not relate here. Some are not so pertinent to this memoir. Others are matters of heart and community that are more personal, and need to be honored with privacy. But there are important, and even critical aspects of this experience that are central to my own spiritual journey, and perhaps for that of others. As I have stated in other parts of this reflection, moments of grace are highly subjective; can't be proved to others; and can be viewed by others with skepticism, even contempt. Those are never reasons enough not to tell one's own story. Enough said as a nod to the great mystery of what is Real, and what is not.

My own vision quest was to be a one-night passage. I had begun fasting before I went out, and only had some water during the quest itself. The setting was a beautiful Texas hill country ranch, with limestone ridges, stands of juniper and oak, meadows for various livestock, and small creeks or "arroyos," meandering through: a very fine blend of native scenery and ranching design. With help from two supporters, I set up my tent, put out the circle of twine with prayer-ties, inside which I would stay, and finally, was left alone. Perhaps around ten in the morning, on a beautiful April day, with good weather all around, I began my vision quest.

I am by nature contemplative, though not withdrawn or introverted. So this experience in nature promised to be restful and restorative. And as far as I'm concerned, that is exactly how it turned out. The midday and afternoon was spent observing and listening to the natural world: the changes in light on the landscape; the sounds of birds and the breeze through the trees; and the subtle vibrations of moving energy all around me. The inner world was equally powerful. I meditated on many things, including the phenomenon of opposites in this life, and how we can only know one extreme of a polarity by knowing something of its opposite. The calm, the solitude, and the relative quiet led me to a deep peacefulness, and I was profoundly grateful for my life and this world.

The night hours were relatively uneventful. There was a chill in the air, but I was warm in my sleeping bag. On a couple of occasions, I went outside the circle to relieve myself, but otherwise stayed in the tent, and slept. The nocturnal passage held sounds of small animals, passing images in my imagination, but mostly dreamless rest. I woke to a cold and quiet morning before the light. As I lay on my pallet, I began to hear small movements in the brush, and I could perceive the first faint lifting of the darkness as the dawn approached. Very slowly, the black turned to gray, the forms of nearby trees and brush came to clarity, and the air began to warm. Lighter and brighter grew the sky in the east, 'til the first full force of the sun broke over the ridge and the world was transformed. The overwhelming furnace of our star began to heat and give life to the dormant creation. The air began to be filled with small winged creatures. Dragonflies, hummingbirds, moths, butterflies, and many others I could not identify, gave my little campsite a buzzing and bountiful energy. The sounds of life around me were constant and made me happy. What power and light! What creativity and abundance! My heart was filled with joy.

Later, perhaps around nine or ten, I lay on the ground, a bit lightheaded from my fast and anticipated the coming of my supporters around noon. I had had no contact with humans, and thus no talking. My mind seemed clear and undisturbed. Off to the side of me, at a distance of several yards, I perceived some movement. Whatever it was, it came on slowly towards me. As it drew closer, I could see the form of a four-legged creature about the size of a small dog. It appeared to be following a natural pathway through the juniper and over the limestone. It stopped. Perhaps it saw the color of my tent. Perhaps it saw me. Whatever the case, it retreated a few steps and found a path slightly above me on the stone ledges of the hillside. I could still perceive its movements through the trees as it slowly came into a cleared space between myself and whatever it was. I thought it might have been a small dog, until I actually clearly saw it.

A beautiful fox!

Bushy tail, small paws, whiskers around its narrow snout. What a fine and fantastic creature. Once again, I was filled with wonder and joy. Nature had given me a particular blessing here, and I knew a certain reverence. The creature stopped, and we exchanged a long, respectful gaze. My world was altered. Gratitude was my dominant feeling.

It is important to note that my last name is Futch, based on the German name Fuchs. In genealogy records, Fuchs is indeed the family name of the European ancestors on my father's side. The translation of this word into English is: Fox! Later, as I related my experience to my mentors, I noted that I had a very fine vision quest, but no flashing lights or angels, but instead a most important visitor. Will related to me: "Greg, not everyone has their family totem come to visit them." I knew I had been richly blessed.

The meaning of this event is inexplicable. You could say it is ineffable. I know I felt a very strong sense of communion with something much greater than myself. I felt the Presence of the Sacred.

My third and final story revolves around a trip with my son to the canyon country of southern Utah. The occasion was my sixtieth birthday. A visit with my son to such a glorious and powerful landscape is, in itself, a time of grace. And I feel that the small event that concludes this chapter is just a part of the larger story of grace in my life.

I had always wanted to see the slot canyon country of Utah. In terms of beauty, mystery, and dramatic form, this country is as good as any other for me. I will not attempt here to give any truly worthy description of this landscape. I believe only poets and the great nature writers can even come close. Suffice it to say, these lands can be harsh, with little extensive vegetation, and trees often restricted to waterways. Hot and usually dry, the wind, the rain, and the sun are the sculptors that shape these magical canyons, mesas, and strange rock formations. The "slots" can be up to 200 feet or more below the bare stretches of sandstone or limestone. They are often very colorful and striated in geologic profusion. If there is a storm, the slot canyons can fill with water quickly, and can trap and drown any hikers unfortunate to be caught unawares.

Grand Staircase Escalante, a national monument, was our destination. Matt flew from Denver, and I from Austin, and we met in Flagstaff. From there, we drove north toward Utah. We stayed in accommodations near the entrance to the monument, and spent the day each day hiking and driving wherever we liked. Only a few roads traverse this preserve, but the places to hike are numerous and intriguing. Near the end of our stay, I chose a slot canyon hike that begins at an access point called, "Wire Pass," and enters a lengthy gorge named, "Buckskin Gulch." Our intention was not to do a long daylong trek, but just go enough to get a sense of the wonder of this beautiful canyon.

And wonderful it was. Steep-sided, narrowing to a few feet in places, and widening into sunny washes at others, this canyon fulfilled our expectation of stone and depth, light and beauty. Matt and I stopped at one point to eat a snack and quench our thirst. There was a fine and deep silence. We drank both water and solitude.

Somewhere a good ways up the canyon, the sound of movement caught my attention. Soon, I could make out a bird flying down the gorge. A single bird, its wings creating a rhythmic pulse, soared steadily toward us. At maybe a hundred yards, it approached us, then flew directly over our heads, and continued its journey toward the next turn in the stone. Just beneath the lip of the canyon, either a crow, or its cousin, the raven, silent except for the flapping of its wings, steady and powerful, slowly it carried on and out of sight.

Spontaneously, my son said, "Well, that didn't happen for no reason!" He had felt the magic also.

In my case, ever since I heard crows cawing over the woods and fields of South Georgia, I have considered them a kind of ally. They remind me of my youth, of the wild, of time, and of that which is timeless.

I will always be most humbly grateful for my son's company, for the slot canyons of Southern Utah, and for that black bird flying so close over our heads.

The natural world can be experienced as a manifestation of the Divine. Nothing new here: this view has been put forth by sages, teachers, and artists throughout human history. And this intuition is so fundamental to who I am that I consider it a way of knowing similar to faith. Furthermore, nature can be communed with. Whether in the sounds of birds, the smell of dirt or blood, the feel of running water, green grass, or granite rock—anyone can experience an interaction beyond words or concepts, which is the definition of communion. Perhaps, one must be open or receptive—like a child—to truly feel and know this communion, but it is a Reality. There are lessons, messages, even little gifts, all of which can be viewed as either personal or impersonal in their Origin.

There is an ongoing dynamic of growth, competition, cooperation, death and ensuing new life that is evident to any observer of natural systems. This dynamic of balance, of cycles, of inter-dependence—often described as an "ecosystem," which is majestic and mesmerizing. For many, it is a continuing display of wonder and grace. There is a profound intelligence and creativity at work here, which—while working through whatever material forces like genes, evolution, and adaptation—cannot be simply reduced to what we call: "material." And, adding my voice to so many others, these dynamics, balances, and systems are not ultimately random or without meaning.

Finally, I would say that humans are an integral part of Nature, but not the master or controller of it. Humanity can shape natural systems, and bring about radical changes on earth—as has already been shown. But human beings are also fundamentally inter-dependent with the natural world. And there is deep hubris and ignorance in the idea that we can either live somehow apart from nature, or in full control of its many dynamics. Humans are not even in full control of themselves! Still, many believe we could ultimately control the natural world. For me, this is a form of madness.

So Rich the Green

So rich the green,
the trees and bushes
breathing outside my window.

The power and the beauty
shines into my soul,
and aliveness gently and
wondrously waves at me.

As dappled light plays
through needles and stems,
and slight breeze ripples leaves
without end,
all feels growth and summer.

The awesome display grows still
as the day lengthens,
and my mind calms in return.

The inward and the out
reach towards each other,
and peace arrives in silence.

EIGHT

Pilgrim, Part 1

My grandparents were very fine people. Mom's mother and father were good Georgia Methodists. They were honest and decent people who worked hard as farmers, raised four children, and as I mentioned earlier, led singing and musical events in their rural community. I thought highly of Maggie and D.E. Newberne and enjoyed going to visit them. Maggie was more reserved and soft spoken, while "Big Daddy" tended to be jolly and outgoing. They both had a sense of humor, and they also shared a strong spiritual faith. They were not evangelical, but their faith strengthened them and gave meaning to their lives. In being such steady and healthy influences, my grandparents helped raise me.

So it is important for this meditation to speak of my diplomatic disagreement with them over a central matter of Christian conviction. Jesus says in John's gospel:

> *"I am the way, and the truth, and the life;*
> *no one comes to the Father, but by me"*
>
> John 14:6

Traditionally, in the Christian faith, this has been interpreted to mean that Jesus Christ is the only way to God—the only channel, the only savior. Sometime in my late high school or first college years, I began to really doubt this particular belief. In my mind and heart, I agreed that Jesus was a true teacher of God, and even one capable of enabling salvation. I was not sure of the "only Son of God" belief, but I deeply honored and revered Jesus, and felt he was an authentic representative of divinity, if not necessarily divine himself. (What does that mean exactly, anyway?) At the same time, I could no longer believe he was the only path to God.

All those other people of faith and good will—even some agnostics and atheists—could not just be consigned to some cosmic junkyard, much less an eternal punishment. All those Muslims and Hindus and Native Americans and Jews and Buddhists and on and on—just summarily dismissed to permanent exile from God? As I felt then, and still feel in so many ways: the God represented by that kind of judgment is just not the God I can have faith in. So, in stating that belief to my grandparents, I made one of my first significant faith statements which was contrary to the beliefs of people I loved. I remember this interaction pretty well. They were hurt, but not condemning, and said something about doing more study and prayer on the issue. Maybe a few more talks with clergy!

This relatively early stand I took came to be somewhat representative of my spiritual journey. I was not content to accept received wisdom if it seemed to contradict either the vision of a benevolent God, or if it ran counter to repeated human experience. From early on in my life, there was a strong impulse to search for truth, in an ultimate sense. As I described in an earlier chapter, science persuaded me that its rigor and discipline could lead to greater knowledge. At the same time, over time I came to see it as a limited tool, and by its own assumptions of what can be real, science totally neglected inner human experience. This area was left to what many considered the dubious field of psychology, or worse, spirituality, not a science at all! Beyond that dimension of reality, science limited itself to what can be detected, measured, or in some way be considered *tangible*. That which is beyond our human senses, or the reach of our instruments, is basically unreal, until some measuring device can "prove" its existence. Consciousness itself remains one of science's major challenges.

Over the years, the spiritual quest became central in my life. The various steps on this quest are the subject of this chapter, and its sequel, later in the memoir. But just to state clearly, an early intuition, and a growing conviction, I began to suspect that all of the great religions, all the wisdom traditions, could be pointing toward the same ultimate and ineffable reality. Many have come to the same conclusion, and in my case, the possibility had to be investigated, explored, and, one could say, *tested!* (A presumptuous idea for some, but many teachers have said not to take their word, but to see for oneself.) The intuition, the growing conviction, that the different paths lead to the same goal, is not really new, it is just that it seems a more widely held feeling than it was in past human history.

Like many thousands of others, in my yearning for understanding and insight, I studied the Eastern traditions and teachers. The Buddha was perhaps the first teacher of the Orient I read carefully. Soon, I had read the Tao, the *Bhagavad-Gita,* the Vedas, and the stories of the Sufis. Each of these sources of wisdom touched something deep inside of me. Listening to a Hindu or Buddhist sage, I felt I was drinking deeply from a spiritual fountain. Over time, I would also return to learn more from the Abrahamic traditions which included my Christian faith, Islam, and Judaism. For all these traditions, it was the *practice*s as well as the beliefs which drew me on. Whether it was meditation, or mindfulness, or centering prayer, the various spiritual disciplines impressed me, and led me to try them with various degrees of commitment. And in my "experiments" with these various spiritual disciplines, even a short and shallow practice convinced me that there was profound truth in the differing paths.

Using Buddhism as a first example, whenever I honestly worked at mindfulness, I could see much more clearly the motions of my thoughts, the restless emotions tied to these thoughts, the presumptions and the biases I carried around, mostly unconsciously. These were very important insights, and they yielded tidbits of self-knowledge which have proven invaluable in whatever progress I make in moral and spiritual awareness. Further, these insights came to also confirm the link between self-knowledge and a deeper view into Reality itself. All of Reality is interdependent, so greater clarity regarding any part of it leads to greater consciousness about the Whole. "Know thyself" is on the Delphic oracle, and Plato has Socrates using it in various contexts. The Sufi poet and mystic Ibn Arabi is quoted in the work, *Kernel of the Kernel,* the following:

> *"To know God is not an easy matter,*
> *until one becomes a knower of one's self."*

There was an intuition, a suspicion of this truth, in my own heart, long before I could think of it concretely. I believe my own interest in psychology, which was my college major, was part of this same intuition. Being raised in the west, and with western categories of thought, psychology was the subject taught in universities which came closest to older traditions (like the Greek or Indian) of self-inquiry. And the narrow focus of western psychology at the time I studied it also explains why I began to lose interest in graduate school. I was looking for more than what I was being taught in abnormal, social, or physiological psychology—all courses I had in either undergraduate or grad school.

As the quote above from Ibn Arabi indicates, another example of sensing the validity of other paths and practices was my study of, and attraction to, Sufi practice and wisdom. There is no end to what could be stated about this profound tradition. The conventional teaching is that Sufism represents the mystical aspect of Islam, and this seems supported by most history and testimony through the ages. First of all, this is a devotional path of loving God, and being loved by God. Thus, the heart and compassion are central in Sufi teaching. From the first time I started reading about Sufism, I was drawn to it, and came to believe it was an authentic path to the Ultimate Reality. The teaching stories, the biographies of Sufi masters recorded here and there, all struck chords deep inside me. And once I had decided there was more than one way to the Divine, I never worried, or doubted, that the same Ultimate Reality was being celebrated, spoken about, worshipped, and loved. In this tradition, as in my childhood Christianity, or Judaism, or Hinduism, human limitations and cultural differences were sure to produce varied experiences and insights into the Infinite. Furthermore, the uses of music and dance in many Sufi circles was, for me, another confirmation that communion with Higher Reality is not primarily, or even most importantly, through the intellect or what we think of as the mind. The human being is a complex living system of many dimensions, many kinds of awareness, and many channels of perception.

But I am getting ahead of my story. Although I had read some Buddhist and Sufi material before I moved to Austin, it was there that I sought out and encountered many other spiritual traditions. At some point I had read *Autobiography of a Yogi,* by Paramahansa Yogananda, and eventually was exposed to the great Indian master, Ramakrishna. In Ramakrishna's life and teaching, I found a description of a path I seemed to be already following, though in an unsophisticated and even simplistic manner. This great saint and devotee of the Hindu deity, Kali, was one of the first teachers I clearly heard state that every authentic religious tradition was pointing to the same final Truth, no matter how mysterious and multifaceted that Truth is. As he is quoted in a book of his sayings:

"Different creeds are but different paths to reach the one God. Diverse are the ways that lead to the temple of Mother Kali at Kalighat in Calcutta. Similarly various are the paths that take men to the house of the Lord. Every religion is nothing but one of these paths."

Sayings of Sri Ramakrishna, p. 149
Sri Ramakrishna Math, Mylapore, Madras, India 1971

During my time in Austin, I spent hours discussing spirituality with a variety of friends and acquaintances. One of them lent me a book about and by Swami Vivekananda, a direct disciple of Ramakrishna. In these pages, and in my conversations with the friend who lent me the book, I found a confirmation of my own faith and experience. There would be too much for me to write about regarding the teachings therein, but suffice it to say here, that the impact on my life of this tradition, and of the essays on Karma, Raja, Jnana and Bhakti Yoga, fed a hunger inside which I knew had everything to do with the Divine. I did not become a devotee of Ramakrishna, but he indeed became one of my primary teachers.

The same friend who gave me the Vivekananda book was talking with me one day and mentioned he had met some people in Austin who followed the Christian path, but who were open to the wisdom of the other great Religions. This would have been sometime in the early 1970s. I decided to investigate these folks. They turned out to be members of the Holy Order of MANS, a semi-monastic group who ran youth hostels, soup and sandwich shops, and lived together as a committed spiritual community. Over a period of years, I spent time with this group, and felt there were some positive and admirable virtues and practices which they upheld. The full members took vows of poverty, humility, obedience, chastity, and service. Their founder had organized the HOOM in ways similar to Catholic orders like the Jesuits and Franciscans. They fasted, gathered for regular worship services, held assets in common, and wore outfits which appeared monastic or clerical. When I came to know them, they were operating a youth hostel in Austin. I had many conversations with the members, and found them to be articulate, dedicated, and serious about the spiritual calling.

This organization, like any other I came to know over time, had its pros and cons. There were people I came to regard as very compassionate and wise, and others I felt were naive and even immature. On the whole, I felt they were genuine in their work and their intentions, and I came to respect the integrity of many members. They ordained women and were an early religious group to take ecological concerns seriously. Both of these aspects were important to me. But their acceptance and honoring of other wisdom traditions was particularly attractive. The youth hostel, as far as I could tell, was run in an efficient and friendly manner.

But there were many problematic elements of the Order's existence. There was no connection to any other Christian denomination or tradition, and therefore their legitimacy, or doctrinal orthodoxy was always suspect. There was no lineage from older established religious organizations. Their founder and his supporters had to a large extent made up a mixture of Masonic, New age, and Christian thought. Many of the beliefs and doctrines were not out of the mainstream of religious culture at large. But it was definitely an esoteric and complex system of teachings which often did not seem to be fully coherent.

Still, the integrity and compassionate nature of many of these people was real and true, in my view. And their personal lives and practices reflected their commitment. After my later move back to Atlanta, Georgia, I continued an association with the Order, and took some discipleship courses. In Atlanta they operated a soup and sandwich restaurant and had a large house where many of them lived. I got to know several of them more personally, and once again, as in Austin, felt an authenticity and devotion to Something Greater, which I agreed with and admired. The members came from many different backgrounds, and included people from Jewish, Christian, and non-religious origin families.

Over time, I realized there were too many of the same issues one finds in any group—egos, lack of sufficient clarity and direction, and some totally unrealistic expectations—for me to be able to commit myself to their path. But as an article I found from an author who researched them in an evenhanded way put it:

"...the Order's history stands as a clear example of how new religious communities are shaped by their surrounding cultural environment. Blighton's mystical, non-sectarian and universalist spiritual vision reflected the innovative, tolerant, and experience-seeking mood of the 1960s and 1970s."

www.wrs.vcu.edu/profiles/HolyOrderOfMans.htm
Accessed 0/2/2015

So, it can be seen from the preceding paragraphs that my search was influenced by the readings I pursued, but also by the people and the communities I encountered. This has been the way for most seekers, and I am no exception. From my Methodist upbringing, to the counter-cultural friends I lived with, to the Holy Order, to Buddhist groups and leaders, and then to churches and groups I will discuss later, my journey followed an old pattern. In all the authentic traditions I have explored, there is the repeating structure of leader, and teaching, and community. So, as with the Buddhists, it is the Buddha, the Dharma, and the Sangha. In Christianity, one could say it is Jesus Christ, the gospel, and the church. The community—the circle of practitioners, worshipers, or disciples—is as critical to the seeker's growth, as is the leader or the teaching. One might be in necessary solitude for some of one's journey, but for the great majority of spiritual searchers, the community is where much of the hard lessons of forgiveness, vulnerability, love, and discipline are worked through. This gathering of fellow travelers, young and old, with different degrees of commitment, becomes the crucible in which accountability and support are deepened. Character, morality, and compassion are all nurtured and tested in the intentional fellowship. As Richard Rohr wrote on page 74 in his fine book, *Falling Upward:*

> *"A crucible, as you know, is a vessel that holds molten metal in one place long enough to be purified and clarified. Church membership requirements, church doctrine, and church morality force almost all issues to an inner boiling point, where you are forced to face important issues at a much deeper level to survive as a Catholic or a Christian, or even as a human. I think this is probably true of any religious community if it is doing its job. Before the truth 'sets you free,' it tends to make you miserable."*

So the community is integral to the spiritual journey, but it is also true that one might be in very different communities in the course of one's life. My pilgrimage is a definite case in point. Each of the "congregations" I have been a part of has broadened my awareness and opened my heart. Every one of these circles has mirrored back to me my own strengths and limitations, and each one, I humbly believe, has been affected, in some way, by my participation.

Following the passing of my father in 1978, my wife and I, and six year old son Matthew, moved back to Atlanta, Georgia. I took a job with Delta Air Lines, and Margaret went through the training to become a Montessori teacher. Asking the reader's patience, this is a good point in the narrative to tell a story of trouble I had in Austin, which is very relevant to my employment by the airline. The conflict I had in Austin gave me insight and even compassion for many people who have been in similar troubles. So the story is tied to events both earlier in my life, and what was about to happen upon our return to Atlanta. So first, here is the story of the trouble.

Margaret and I were living in a rental house in Austin with our son Matthew, who was about age 1 at the time. This would thus be about 1973 or 1974. Our neighbors were a Hispanic family with several children, some still living at home. One day not long after we moved into our rental house, I was sitting in the dining area, while Matt sat on the floor in front of me. I began to hear a few pinging sounds, like a rock hitting a metal plate. I looked up at one of the windows, and as I focused on it, something struck the glass pane, and caused a small shatter. The window pane did not fall apart, but the glass was broken. It took me a moment to realize what was happening: some sort of projectile was hitting our window. And it seemed to be the kind fired out of a gun.

As Matthew was sitting only a few feet from the window, I jumped up and ran to see what was happening. Our lot had a dirt driveway between our property and the neighbors'. Their house had a sort of enclosed porch on the side facing our house, and the walls were boarded in a somewhat haphazard manner. Someone in that addition was apparently shooting at our windows. I ran through the door facing the driveway, and without much hesitation ran into their back yard. As I did, a boy maybe 14 ran out the door of the porch and headed for the back door of the house proper. I caught up to him, and grabbed him by the shoulders, and shouted, "What are you doing?!"

Quickly, his family members came out of the house, and I told them what had happened. The upshot of the incident is that they charged me with trespassing! To make a very long story short, the case went to trial, and since the boy was a minor, and I just wanted to tell my story and defend myself, there was no separate hearing to charge him. I hired an attorney, and he did a good job of presenting my case, and my brother gave positive testimony concerning my character. The judge was very sympathetic to my story, and demanded the family produce the gun—a pellet rifle—which they did and admonished them for not monitoring their son's reckless behavior. But the judge ruled I was guilty of "simple assault by contact" for grabbing the boy—a misdemeanor—and fined me all of $2.50!

As I think back now—over 35 years later—to how I felt about this discouraging event, it seems that confusion, resignation, and some simple acceptance, were some of my reactions. The lack of fairness was clear to me, but I did not feel this was such a damaging event that my future life would be held hostage to it. And finally, I am not sure what all I felt and thought. One thing I am sure of is how this incident made me more sensitive to the random injustices throughout a nation supposedly devoted to "law and order." From racial differences in prosecution and incarceration, to disproportionate enforcement of laws targeting powerless people over the rich and well connected, to the way police forces, and the FBI and other agencies, often become tools against legitimate dissent, the list reflected my own worries and anger about our society. But their importance was emphasized by my trouble in Austin.

Now, to connect this story to my past, present, and future, I'll ask the reader to recall how I mentioned in Chapter 3 that I was part of a Boy Scout troop in Atlanta. One of the important figures in this troop was about to play an important role in our life in 1978, the year of my father's passing. It happened that I was able to get a job interview with Delta Air Lines in Atlanta. There would be two talks, and the first one went fine. On my application, I had described the Austin conflict, not wanting to hide it from any background check. As I walked into the room where my final interview was to take place, the man waiting there was my old Boy Scoutmaster! I could not believe it.

We had a very good conversation, catching up with each other's lives, and then he turned to the application. Pointing at the story of the Texas incident, he asked "So, Greg, what happened in this Austin problem you had?" I carefully related the story, just as I have just done here, and at the end of the telling, this wise gentleman said something like, "OK, don't worry about it." And I got the job. This man knew a lot about my family, and my history. I'm sure he figured this was not a representative example of who I was.

Many events in our lives are linked to many others. This was a particularly good example of that reality.

Now returning to the chronological narrative, this Atlanta chapter of our lives was difficult for many reasons. My mother's drinking was central. Though she would have stretches of normality, the loss of my father's stabilizing influence led to bouts of intoxication which might last a day or more. We lived in close proximity, and visited regularly, and Mom would sometimes baby-sit Matt. But she was not completely reliable, and this led to times of heartache and anger for Margaret and me. She was an inconsistent influence on our lives, and so our feelings were decidedly mixed. Margaret's teaching positions were demanding, and she struggled with keeping parents and administrators satisfied. Her love for children, however, was the big positive in her work. My own work at the airline was, in the beginning, manual labor, both at the maintenance facility, and on the ramp. Later, I was to move upstairs to the terminal and gates, and worked in public contact for about ten years. I was glad, however, that I had a good job, with decent pay, with benefits of medical coverage for the family, vacation time, and the ability to fly on passes.

We searched for a church where we might feel comfortable, and attended more than one Methodist congregation, before we settled on Trinity United Methodist in downtown Atlanta. Trinity UMC is an old and venerable institution, and has a rich heritage of social justice ministry, and when we were there, benefited from a membership which included retired missionaries, ministers, and academics. We were members during the 1980s, and some of its outreach programs included a large soup kitchen operation on Sundays, a cold weather overnight shelter serving men, and various other ministries focused on poor neighborhoods in the inner city. Margaret came to feel at home at this church and sang in the choir. I helped in various ways at Trinity, with the soup kitchen, and sometimes with the night shelter. But my favorite activity was the Sunday school program for adults, and I led several classes while we were members there.

Probably the most significant event of this time period with regard to my spiritual journey, was the decision to enter seminary at Emory University in Atlanta. I had been having theological discussions with a young man who was already attending the seminary, and who was the son of a Methodist clergyman himself. Over time, we became friends, and he played a part in my decision to enter Candler School of Theology. My friend was Rev. Dan Wilson, and he was an associate pastor at the Methodist church my folks attended. My parents had known his parents from south Georgia days. One day, Dan invited me to a dinner he was going to share with an Emory professor. I was intrigued and curious, and so was glad to accept. The professor turned out to be Dr. James Fowler, an important academic with a focus on what he termed the stages of faith. These theoretical stages seemed reflected in research work done with people of different ages and inspired many human development academics and also counselors and ministers. The proposed stages were similar in some ways to Piaget's levels of child development, and to Kohlberg's theories of moral growth.

I had a very good time with Dan and Dr. Fowler, and I just remember one of the concluding remarks from the professor. To paraphrase his question, he asked, "Well Greg, how are we going to keep you *out* of seminary?" This question, and the richness of our discussions seemed to do the trick. In the year 1981, I began attending the school of theology, while working full time for Delta Air Lines. I would usually take 2 courses per semester, and many of my work shifts were in the evening, so my mornings were free for classes. But it was a very demanding, and stressful path. With a wife and young son, I found my days and evenings fully booked, and, like my wife, grew weary many times over. At the same time, I was drawn to the subject matter and the work, of the seminary training, and found the process to be deeply enriching. I was forced to grow in many ways, and I was already engaged in the messy project of maturing, since being just a decent spouse and father requires it!

It would take me *ten years* to complete my Master of Divinity degree at Emory. Normally, this was a three year project, but I was working full time, and did the best I could. My advisors and the administration were supportive of my long journey, and basically, I just had to maintain a steady progress, and an adequate grade point average, to be allowed to soldier on. There were many fine teachers, advisors, and mentors, during this time, too many to list. But it is important for me to mention a few. One of my favorites was Dr. Fred Craddock, a professor of homiletics (preaching), and a warm and engaging teacher. Prof. Craddock could bring passages of scripture to life in his lessons and his sermons. He was considered by his peers to be one of the finest preachers of his generation. And in the class that I took with him, he was funny, compassionate, and inspiring. It was a privilege to listen to his stories, and his insights into gospel narratives. His sermons followed an "inductive" plan. Put simply, induction is a mode of reasoning which proceeds from examples of experience and moves toward general truths. Deduction, by contrast, does the reverse. So, in one case (deduction), there is a main theme or proposal one wants to make, and which is stated up front, and then one shows how this truth plays out in reality. For inductive preaching, per Craddock, "the immediate and concrete experiences of the people are significant ingredients in the formation and movement of the sermon and not simply the point the final applications and exhortations are joined." *

Thus, Craddock's sermons were full of life and the concrete details of people's daily existence. They tended not to be abstract or dry. And so, most listeners laughed, nodded in recognition of familiar dilemmas, and were moved by the experience of somehow participating in the very message given. This was Fred Craddock at his best. He was a delight in the classroom, and a warm presence to interact with. Prof. Craddock recently passed away and will be greatly missed by those he touched.

Another very important teacher for me, was Dr. Parke Renshaw. Parke was both a part of Candler's supervised ministry program, and a member of my home church, Trinity UMC. Parke had been a missionary in Brazil, and had a special feeling and fondness for Latin American affairs. He was an activist in the best sense of the word, and he was my mentor when I worked with him at the Christian Council of Atlanta, an ecumenical service agency which coordinated many kinds of work in the community. There were clothing banks, and refugee resettlement programs, and social justice outreach programs of many kinds. Parke and I worked together during the time of the Nicaraguan revolution, and the Sandinista-Contra struggles. I felt a part of something important, as we tried to see beyond clichés and Ronald Reagan's support of the Contras. There were battles in Congress over funding the

---

*As One Without Authority, 1979, p. 59

Contras, and many liberal churches opposed the Reagan administration's knee-jerk support of anti-Communist forces. For me, anti-Communist in these circumstances were usually reactionaries, and wanted to return to days of pseudo-colonialism, in which ruling elites keep everyone in their place. And because there was a shared interest between people like the Nicaraguan dictator Anastasio Somoza and anti-communist politicos in the US, the common people on the ground in El Salvador, Guatemala, and Nicaragua were usually just pawns in a bigger game. And they remained poor, oppressed, and without much voice. These were the issues Parke and I and others addressed, in seminars, and outreach programs in churches and other venues. This was a rich experience for me, and I am most grateful I was able to part of it. Parke Renshaw is another mentor who recently passed away and he will remain an admirable and passionate mentor in my journey.

The third person I would like to mention is Dr. Don Saliers. This gentleman was a professor of theology and worship at Candler when I was there. His passion was in showing the relationships between prayer, music and liturgy, and the religious affections like gratitude, repentance, and love. All these elements of the religious life interact with each other. They shape the emotions and the character of both the individual and the worshipping community. Don's enthusiasm was contagious, and for one who loved music and spirituality—like me—his classes were energizing, inspiring, and even providential. In using the word affections, in his book *The Soul in Paraphrase,* Dr. Saliers wanted to emphasize a deeper orientation than is usually implied by the word emotion. When we use the word sentiment or even emotion, there is an implication of transience, superficiality. Saliers wants to write of a more complex and substantial reality which is integral to the person of faith. The following quote from page 11 of his book is relevant:

> *"Questions about emotion and the affections are frequently regarded today as psychological rather than properly theological questions. Emotions essential to religious life and particularly to the practice of prayer are commonly categorized as 'subjective' in the sense of 'private'. To many religious people and to many systematic theologians, the affections do not seem the sort of thing susceptible of being clarified by theological reflection."*

By contrast, his aim in the book is to indeed present a theological investigation of those very affections.

In the context of seminary, this is an important issue. There is much suspicion in theology schools around religious experience and emotions. And there are good reasons to doubt excess zeal and "enthusiasm," which was one of the very insults hurled at the early "Methodists." The wariness with which mysticism is still treated in much western seminary education is a continuation of a certain skepticism regarding both interior experience which can't be "verified," and an uncontrolled emotionalism which may or may not have anything to do with authentic devotion or worship. Don Saliers had both the presence and the depth to wrestle with spirituality and its expression. It is no wonder that his daughter Emily went on to become one-half of the popular "Indigo Girls" music act.

Seminary was a wonderful experience for me, on so many levels. It sharpened my own questions about the One

Who we call God, and exposed me to many other seekers, and fine, wise elders. Seminary forced me to become more articulate, and also to value what gifts I was already trying to offer my community of faith. It was a testing ground for commitment, but also for what seemed my own talents and interests. At the same time, I came to the conclusion I would not be seeking ordination, and that my particular passion was small groups. This was an important insight, and I have continued to work at leading and participating in small gatherings for study, fellowship, and spiritual growth. In and of itself, this service has been a great blessing, for I have definitely received more than I have given.

NINE

Pilgrim, Part 2

Finally, in 1991, I received my Master of Divinity degree from Emory University. No saint wore that cap and gown—but I was happy to complete the long journey. I believed this credential would allow me to teach classes and to listen with compassion to those who trusted me enough to share their struggle. I would also be able to continue my own spiritual pilgrimage with a bit more self-awareness.

Self-awareness is a cornerstone—a pre-requisite for further growth. But it is also a never-ending process. Seeing deeply into one's own fears, secret places, motivations and dreams is, unquestionably, a life-long pursuit. Humans not only have the unique ability to deceive ourselves, we definitely don't want to look much into our "shadow" side. We avoid and refuse to acknowledge the areas and dimensions of our lives that represent the dark side of our personalities. These voices and drives within us either make us feel ashamed or fearful, or we may think we have outgrown or "transcended" them. Any sincere seeker must do difficult inner work. This inner practice, combined with the challenge of life itself, produces a form of discipline.

Many forms of discipline exist, and many forms of practice are integral to them all, which means commitment and persistence on our part.

I was clear that I was not pursuing ordination into a particular denomination. I never saw the seminary degree as an income-producing instrument. But I was also not convinced that my own faith could fit neatly into any of the mainline Christian churches. So why go there? I wondered. I knew I wanted to do something more with my life than just work toward retirement from the airline. At that time in 1994, Central Texas seemed to be calling both Margaret and me.

My main concern was my mother. My father had been gone for over 15 years. However, my Mom had stopped drinking—a major blessing to herself and all who cared about her. In fact, AA and the love and support of family and friends had played a major part in her ability to stop drinking in the mid-1980s. So, her bag of AA chips was already beginning to fill up!

Born Ferry Wynell Newberne, my mother was turning age 69 in the year we considered moving back to the Lone Star state. My brother Ronnie was living with her in the same house the family had occupied since high school days. Mom seemed to be getting along well, but there were many questions and doubts I wrestled with before making a final decision about moving. It is well known to many that Alcoholics Anonymous adopted what is called the "Serenity Prayer" as a source of wisdom and comfort. I knew it myself from AA meetings I attended with my mother. The prayer's best-known form is:

> *God grant me the serenity to accept the things*
> *I cannot change,*
> *The courage to change the things I can,*
> *And the wisdom to know the difference.*

These lines have often come to mind for me during hours of stress, indecision, or sorrow. Serenity, courage, and wisdom are all exemplary qualities. If I had to choose one as most critical, it would probably be wisdom.

So in my meditation over leaving my airline job and moving away from my aging parent, I prayed for wisdom. I've always considered intuition, and even what we call "the conscience," to be aspects or sources of wisdom. Intuitively, I felt that my life needed to be about more than a secure job. I also knew that the return to Texas was about answering some call from deep within. This was a necessary transition in my life—one that represented a variety of other turning points of my journey.

Although I am by no means a regular risk-taker, the decision to leave Delta Air Lines is a good example of my priorities at that time. Security in the "material world" has long seemed an illusion to me. There is no ultimate safety—or true fulfillment—in the goals, or the "idols" of this world. Whether it was money, power, sex, or prestige, the popular values of culture became more and more empty to me as I grew up. Even at an early age, my yearning was for something deeper, lasting, and more authentic.

I have already briefly discussed how Buddhism has helped me in my own journey, but even before I had read or heard the Buddha's teachings, I must have felt the truth of words I saw later in the Pali Canon:

"Decay is inherent in all component things!
Work out your salvation with diligence."

Suttapitaka Mahaparinibbana-sutta, 6:10

This seems a brutal, cold, and impersonal view. And yet, for me, there was a profound truth there.

Several people questioned my leaving the airline job, although a few said they envied me. The decision to move 1,000 miles from my mother was perhaps a little more complex. I could produce a list of reasons, but it all came down to my decision that this was a manifestation of truly "leaving home." Though concerned for my mother, I knew my brother, a church community, AA friends, and others would all help keep track on her. *I can always fly home if necessary,* I reassured myself.

We made the momentous move to Austin. I took a job with a start-up company focused on travel. Margaret continued her teaching in a Montessori school. I wanted to find a church community where I could settle in and my search brought me to Trinity United Methodist church. It is a liberal and reconciling congregation and its pastor, Sid Hall, is a progressive Protestant minister. Perhaps his most passionate cause is LGBT issues. He always revealed to me an ecumenical spirit and has been very involved in various social justice efforts. These two dimensions of religious life—ecumenism and justice struggles—were always integral to my own journey. Relieved I'd found a church home, I began to get involved in congregational activities.

At Trinity, I was able to engage my seminary training and my love of small groups. Over the years I was a member there, I was able to lead and be a part of many classes, discussions groups, and prayer and fellowship gatherings. Each of these experiences broadened my own awareness, opened my heart, and honed my humble skills at working with smaller groups of people. I have often found there is an optimum number of participants in which all can both contribute and learn from others. For me, the best number is between 6 and 15, but that is, of course, an ideal.

As I mentioned in a previous chapter, at some point in my Trinity UMC sojourn, I asked Sid Hall for some references, as I was looking for a spiritual guide or mentor. Sid graciously took no offense at my not asking him to be my guide and suggested three people. From this conversation came my association with Will Taegel, sweat lodges, vision quests, and a community open to spiritual growth and healing. I have already given a brief description of Will and Judith and their work creating and guiding the "Earthtribe" community.

I know for a fact that this community is an authentic fellowship for emotional and spiritual nourishment. The three main practices—sweats, vision quests, and the Earthdance—are carefully planned and carried out. Safety and accountability are integral to these rituals.

Each practice has value and each one can potentially stretch the participant beyond his or her comfort zone. It is my experience and my observation that this community and their practices can trigger healing, growth, and deep insight into oneself and one's world. One of the other important characteristics of Will and Judith's work is their openness to wisdom from the various great religions. There is acceptance of truth in Buddhist, Jewish, Sufi, and Christian traditions, as well as indigenous worldviews, like those of North American native tribes. It should be obvious by now that his recognition of wisdom from non-Christian sources was particularly attractive to me.

During my roughly ten-year stay at Trinity UMC in Austin, I led quite a few classes and discussion groups, as I have noted before. Some of these were focused on either the different world religions, or on common practices shared among the various traditions. One of these classes looked at the history of "sweat lodges," or sweat baths, from Roman, Siberian, Scandinavian, Turkish, and North American native perspectives. I spent most of the series on the work of Will and Judith. It was called, "The Sweat Lodge as Therapy Tool," and I enjoyed preparing material for the class, and sharing what I had found with the group. It was a popular class, usually averaging 10 to 15 people, and I believe it spoke to a variety of interests, longings, and concerns held by the attendees.

It is difficult to articulate what the sweat lodge experience is like, and the effects it has upon participants. The Earthtribe sweats were always "healing sweats" when I was attending them. That is, they entailed prayers, chants, singing, and an atmosphere of fellowship and support. They were not "warrior sweats." And the sensory experience of the heat, the incense and the water on the rocks, are all central to a feeling of purging, of a bodily cleansing. The mind, the emotions, and the body—all parts of our integral being—are effected in the sweat lodge.

"Getting out of the head," might be a way of describing this ritual. In general, the experience develops a greater awareness that true learning, growth, or transformation must involve the entire human being, not just one part. For example, when learning to swim, there is no substitute for being in the water, and feeling the complete body/mind involvement of moving through and coming to a harmonious interaction with that water. And so it goes with most of what we learn in this life. The actual experience of an interaction with some aspect of reality can touch the emotions, the physical sensations, the mind dynamics, and the development of skills necessary to "learn" what is needed. Learning in the mind alone is often not real learning at all. It is an accumulation of intellectual knowledge, with the attendant mental models, and even emotional attitudes that go with that mind experience. It may not touch the deeper levels of our total being, which must be activated to achieve actual growth.

My point here is not to downplay or ignore the profound need for intellectual or mental work and learning. It is obvious how critical for civilization are the disciplines of mathematics, medical research, science in general, and so many more. These endeavors all are dependent on basic intellectual knowledge, and our world would not exist as it is without them. My argument here is that the human being grows, learns, matures, and one could say "evolves" through experiences that engage the total person: consciousness, emotional dynamics, and the physical body itself. This is much too large an issue for my memoir to tackle. Suffice it to say that I believe all true spiritual growth—the most profound kind—happens when the total person is involved. It is not primarily a matter of cognitive or mental knowledge or advancement. For those who believe in them, the heart and the soul must be engaged!

Thus, like so many others, I have long ago concluded that the most critical areas of human development only come about through changes in human awareness and the emotional and spiritual "capacities." The necessary movement towards a one-planet consciousness, the recognition of climate change and our adaptation to it, and the actual evolution of human "nature" are all dependent on "growing up," becoming more mature creatures—in short, on evolving! The dynamics of human growth, especially in awareness of life's interdependence, the requirements of living in harmony with each other and the natural world, and in realizing what gives ultimate meaning and worth to a person's life—all these are inextricably interwoven with each other, and one aspect does not advance without the others.

For true awareness to be possible, we must be able to see that a consumerist, materialist lifestyle is ultimately both futile for happiness, and incredibly destructive to the very natural environment that sustains our lives. In so many ways, this seems very obvious and clear, but the journey to accepting the implications of these points is usually long and often painful.

My intention in this book is to limit the focus to these two critical themes: (1) the need to change our awareness of and relationship to, Nature, and (2) the spiritual growth, which is both our opportunity in this life, and the only final way to what we call happiness. I believe these two callings are intimately tied together. I do not claim that a person must have any conventional religious beliefs or outlook, however, there must be some awareness of a Greater Reality. One that makes claims upon our responsibilities, which sustains all life and existence, and which must be reckoned with in some manner for there to be any peace or serenity in our lives.

There are many people who have offered strategies and blueprints for the changes that are coming. Visionaries and prophets of a healthier society and planet include:

Thomas Berry, Bill McKibben, Wendell Berry, Joanna Macy and so many others. For decades, Joanna Macy has taught and written about "The Great Turning," meaning "the shift from the industrial growth society to a life-sustaining civilization (https://www.ecolitercy.org/article/great-turning) Most helpful is her listing of three areas of work needed to help bring about the fundamental changes necessary for the evolution toward sustainability.

The first is: "Actions to slow down the damage to Earth and its beings." She includes examples such as documenting the negative effects of the industrial society, alerting the culture to "illegal and unethical corporate practices," and activism such as conducting vigils at places of ecological destruction. The second is: "Analysis of structural causes and the creation of structural alternatives." One example would be reduction of reliance on fossil fuels, and conversion to renewables. Much work has already been done in this area, and much more remains. The third is: "A shift in consciousness," a fundamental requirement, which runs parallel to and supplements these afore mentioned endeavors. Macy and her work have inspired many who have struggled to remain hopeful and to find ways to assist in changing society.

As we all struggle to find our paths into new ways of living, and healthier relationships with each other, the Creation, and THAT one chooses to see as the Higher Power, we continue to need guides I believe in the saying: When the student is ready, a teacher will appear, but I also believe we must play our own role in finding our guides and mentors. Through my own journey, I have been nurtured and guided by various models of human growth. Some are more psychological, or cognitive. Some are more "spiritual" in tone and language. Many point in the same direction or overlap.

When it comes to the exploration of human growth, I would like to highlight the endeavors of Bill Plotkin. His work has inspired and helped me, and I have led at least two classes on his books. He has added the context of Nature to concepts of human development. This is very important, since, in general, models of growth, especially in the West, do not consider the natural world as a critical "container" in which human maturation takes place. The first of Dr. Plotkin's books, which I read and later led a class on, is *Soulcraft: Crossing into the Mysteries of Nature and Psyche.* I wrote a review of *Soulcraft*, which was printed in a 2007 issue the journal: "The Ecozoic Reader," which reads as follows:

> *"The most profound insights of spirituality cannot be adequately expressed in words. This is an ancient truth. The deepest truths require special means of transmission.... In every spiritual tradition, there are various rituals, pathways, techniques, or 'means of grace', which offer the possibility of contact with Ultimate Reality.*

In his fine book, *Soulcraft*, Bill Plotkin writes about techniques for what he calls: 'soul encounter'. These are methods of altering everyday consciousness so that 'aspects of ourselves hidden from everyday awareness' may be revealed."

Plotkin spends some time discussing how modern, especially American, society has become adolescent in its priorities, values, and goals. He writes on page one of the Introduction of *Soulcraft:*

> *"Contemporary society has lost touch with soul and
> the path to psychological and spiritual maturity, or
> true adulthood. Instead, we are encouraged to create lives
> of predictable security, false normality, material comfort,
> bland entertainment, and the illusion of eternal youth."*

I believe many of us in the world today feel this sense of immaturity and "false idols" in our culture at large. Thus, we are attracted to visionaries like Plotkin, Macy, and Berry, who give us diagnoses of our plight and offer legitimate paths forward.

In his subsequent book, *Nature and the Human Soul,* Plotkin skillfully incorporates many sources of wisdom and insight into a model of human development. This model owes a lot to earlier theories of growth, including those of Piaget, Kohlberg, and Erickson, but more than any of these, it emphasizes the cycles and rhythms of nature, and the writers, poets, and teachers who have focused on them, to give a much more comprehensive vision of human maturation happening within the inextricable context of the natural world. Just as the butterfly only transforms within the cocoon, the human being can only develop in a healthy, whole manner within the greater cocoon of Nature itself.

Briefly stated, Plotkin maps stages of human growth onto a version of the Native American medicine wheel. I have found much to admire in this vision and believe there are profound truths here. There is too much to explore in this vision, so I will just conclude my remarks on Plotkin's work with a look at his introductory statements to *Nature and the Human Soul.* Five facets of the "wheel of life" are proposed as purposes for the model:

1. *A map or story of optimal human development*

2. *.A design tool for creating healthy human communities and life-sustaining societies.*

3. *A portrait of the emerging stage of human evolution.*

4. *A set of guidelines for individual psychological healing and "wholing."*

5. *A deep cultural therapy—a way to heal and transform our existing human cultures.*

There is no lack of ambition in this grand presentation and perhaps a little more humility might be helpful. On the other hand, the absolutely critical dimension of humanity's integration with, dependence on, and ultimate unity with, the Natural World (Mother Earth for short) is given its necessary due in this tremendous work. Good going, Dr. Plotkin!

As I've made clear in various ways, my heart aches for planet Earth, and the mindless ways humans have exploited and degraded it. The living, breathing world of creatures, weather and climate systems, geologies and energies, are all under grave threat now. There is such of roiling mix of melancholy, anger, feelings of helplessness, and grief, that every new outrage produces a numbing sense of inevitability. But of what? Total destruction, extinction of homo sapiens, cataclysms beyond our imaginings?

Perhaps. It is easy to feel that the path is set now and not much can be done to reverse the trashing of our planet.

And yet, no one can predict the dynamics of earth systems and the mysterious, minimally understood ways in which forces of destabilization in one area lead sometimes to new, creative restoring conditions in another. Our physical, natural world is too complex to be certain of anything. We have been wrong so many times in the past, and scientists in particular are wary of sweeping conclusions. Science advances by transcending earlier models of reality, incorporating new evidence. This is not a Pollyanna argument against changing human behavior. It is a realistic statement of the limits of human understanding.

And finally, as this treatise has repeatedly discussed, a Greater Whole is my own conviction and experience. A spiritual reality for me is the ultimate context of our lives. It is, indeed, a great Mystery. But IT does not leave us completely without insights, wisdom, and clues to what is REAL. In the closing essays of this book, I wish to write about two other spiritually inclined guides, and to make final comments on my own journey.

CAN YOU HEAR ME

Are You still with us,
    Mother Earth?

Or is the tide turning,
        the consequences piling up?

Those of us who sense
Love in the Universe

    know it's a sort of
        Tough Love, unsentimental.

So maybe our rapacious ways
    have played out our luck.

Perhaps we've gone too far
    and can't bring it back.

        Can You hear me,
            Mother of us all?

Can You hold out hope
that many see the Writing

    on the Wall, and are
        struggling to change, to

show our respect, to
remember our love for

the beauty, the life-
giving, the freely-given

Nurturing You Are?
We are trying. Please

don't give up on us.
Show us the way,

show us our work.
Forgive our delusions,

our proud belief
we are the masters,

that we control and dominate
the land, the water, the air.

Is it not both comical
and sad to You,

dear Mother, the
blindness and fantasy?

Little creatures we are,
but we plead for

mercy, and pray for
strength, time and character

to learn to "walk humbly,"
and find the communion
with Creation.

May God help us,
Mother Earth.

Recall our frailty,
we plead, and
restore us to health.

TEN

Testament

*From earliest times we have known, if we are willing
to know, having learned by experience and example, that
when people are disconnected from their land they suffer.
But that is only half of the truth. The other half is that
when its rightful people, the people who rightfully
care for it, are absent from it, the land suffers. It is the
mutual, indivisible suffering of land and people
that sets in right perspective the suffering of either.*

Wendell Berry *Our Only World,* p.111

If one looks at reality or history from one perspective,
there might be hope. If looked at from another, there
might be gloom, even despair. I believe many of us vacillate
between one and the other. On the one hand, the evidence
for cultural decline in our country and environmental
decay in our world seems abundant, even undeniable.
On the other hand, one can find counter-vailing trends,
inspiring examples, and reasons for hope on both the
cultural and environmental fronts. But it is such a complex

and bewildering, sometimes conflicting, sometimes cooperating mixture of light and dark, that a summary judgement appears impossible.

In the United States of the twenty-first century, there is a continuing evolution of problematic currents in our society and its values. First of these for me is a materialistic concept of success and happiness. This one has dogged our country, and many others, for a long time. There has always been dissent from this concept, but in the main, "the pursuit of happiness" has had a very physical, materialistic component in American consciousness. This impulse, in a way, has a biological, even genetic basis. The drive for food, water, shelter, and safety is fundamental to living organisms on earth, not just humans. But once people get beyond simple physical survival, then sources of comfort and entertainment become more and more important. And a majority of us have seen material abundance, and also amusement, to be central aspects of happiness and fulfillment.

This is "old news" to those who reflect deeply on the human condition. And this error of materialism as a main source of happiness and fulfillment is compounded and exaggerated by a second, very profound and disturbing trend: the move towards instant gratification. The ability to delay gratification is seen the world over as a sign of maturity, over against the impulse in infants and young children to have needs and wants met RIGHT NOW. It is at least possible that the human desire to find fulfillment as soon as possible will lead to some degree of burnout, satiation, and a search for the deeper sources of happiness. But will the Earth's decreasing bounty endure long enough for humanity to "grow up"?

The long journey of homo sapiens from hunter-gatherers, through agriculture and the rise of civilizations, through the scientific and industrial revolutions, and now towards high-tech robotics and genetic manipulation is seen by most as unqualified progress. But, only in a narrow sense is this history progress. Lives are easier in many ways, but has human nature changed? The dark sides of human dynamics remain as they have been for millennia: unreasoning fear and anxiety, self-centered and ego driven behavior, hostility towards those different from ourselves, bias against, and jingoistic views of, other cultures, and the human tendency to project upon others the negative energies that live within ourselves. Many are the frailties and weaknesses of human nature, and external conditions do not usually alter those in any significant way. The concept of human nature itself is a slippery one. "Human nature" seems more of a label for our conflicting, mysterious inner life, than a definable quality. But risking that major caveat, I believe the core dimensions of human nature include: (1) level and breadth of awareness, (2) insight based on experience, and (3) wisdom about what is real and what is illusory. (One could then argue that one person's human nature is very different from another's.) These inner qualities are not much affected by cultural circumstances or intellectual worldviews.

Experience in life yields insights about complexity, nuance, and the necessity of adjusting one's behavior to the situation at hand. Interacting with a law-enforcement officer requires a quality of seriousness and attention quite different from what is needed to talk with a child. Both are very important interactions, but the particular kind of attention and seriousness is different. The level and breadth of awareness of a mature 70 year old is significantly dissimilar to that of 35 year old. And, as for wisdom, a special virtue partaking of emotional, psychological, and spiritual maturity, one might note, for example, that a wise person knows "what glitters is not always gold!" That is, superficial appearances, however persuasive, often hide the true nature of a situation, a particular person, or a sensory perception. The earth seems flat for anyone just using our human vision and our perspective, standing on the ground. Thus, after this long excursus, it is my summary statement that human beings are very capable of growth in character and wisdom. At the same time there are consequences for our negative, immature and destructive tendencies which might doom us before our better angels can save us.

Our current situation of degrading planet Earth, partly for necessary items like food, water, and shelter, but increasingly for entertainment, excessive consumer greed, and even a kind of permanent distraction from life itself, signals (even screams) that we confront a spiritual crisis. It is a crisis within ourselves, not in scarcity, outside enemies real or imagined, or a malevolent entity (like the devil) beyond time and space. And so, my memoir returns to the beginning. In these days (2018) of stress and confusion, of a US presidency unprecedented in chaos (Donald Trump), of the denial of human assisted climate change, and of many people in many countries wanting to return to an attitude of "us first," of rejecting the immigrant, and a nostalgia for a time that wasn't quite as good as remembered, a sense of futility and nihilism can be very strong. However, in spite of experiencing the power of darkness (or perhaps partly because of it), humanity through the millennia have sensed a Higher Reality, a source of light and meaning, which cannot be overcome. This is my experience.

D. Gregory Futch

In this humble meditation of a memoir, I have tried to describe my own faith journey. Generally speaking, people of faith usually experience both an *awareness,* more mind-based, and *feelings,* more heart-based, with regard to THAT which is revered or worshipped. This Ineffable Reality can be perceived as impersonal, or personal. Our limited human senses, intuitions, and imaginations can only very dimly glimpse aspects of this Reality. But whether one comes from a non-theistic tradition like Buddhism, or a theistic one like Judaism, there is consistent testimony that any person can have some Direct Experience of this Ineffable Reality.

It is probably obvious to the reader by now that I believe there are many paths to communion with the Infinite. I have believed this for many years now. One of the main reasons I was drawn to the life and teachings of Sri Ramakrishna (1836-1866), as I mentioned in the Pilgrim One chapter, is his statement that all faiths are paths to the One God. To this day in the twenty-first century, this is a very minority view, to say the least. And, writing in my own words what this means is important: I conceive of the Higher Power as such a complex and even unfathomable Reality, that each of the major traditions is simply one window on this awesome and even fearsome Mystery. In some schools of Buddhism, the word "suchness" is used to refer to the essential "beyond description or conception" quality of the Infinite. For example, in traditions like Buddhism and Advaita Vedanta, one could say that the Ultimate Truth is that there is only One Unified reality (not-two), and that in general, this Reality is beyond gods and goddesses, (though often including them), beyond concepts like the soul and individual salvation, and even beyond the division between Being and Non-Being! Thus, we just say that everything is "suchness." A far cry from theistic religion, one would say.

However, these very differing traditions have surprisingly similar things to say about human behavior, about meditation, about consciousness, and even about this Final Reality. Only by study and practice will one come to see the Truth of this assertion. Another example of a window on the Great Mystery are the concepts of pantheism and panentheism. Bear with me as I try and explicate in a very superficial way the difference here. According to the second edition of the Encarta Webster's Dictionary, pantheism is "the belief that God and the material world are one and the same thing and that God is present in everything." Of course, the usual objections include "how can cancer be part of God?" or "how was God in Hitler, or serial killers?" But, for now, we are just giving the definition. By contrast, panentheism is the "belief that the divine pervades and interpenetrates every part of the universe" (Wikipedia), but is also beyond all time and space, and thus transcends all created reality. That is, God is somehow integral to all Creation, but is also completely Transcendent to it. So, the Divine is not in any way dependent on created reality but is still at ONE with it. Or, along with the Hindus, one could simply say that God is both immanent and transcendent.

In my time at Trinity UMC in Austin, two books in particular strongly influenced me, and continue to inspire and comfort me. As much as anything else, they affirmed intuitions and convictions I was already moving toward. The two books are *Essential Spirituality,* by Roger Walsh, and *The Mystic Heart,* by Wayne Teasdale. These works share many observations and conclusions. They both illustrate and explicate many of the commonalities found in the world's great religions. And even though I have not met either of these two authors, I consider them mentors on my spiritual path.

In *Essential Spirituality*, Walsh outlines and discusses seven fundamental practices that are common to all the authentic religious traditions. Each of these tasks are overlapping with others, and each might be called by different names in the various traditions. But there are deep insights in this categorization. The practices are: (1) transforming motivations, (2) concentrating and calming the mind, (3) selfless service, (4) cultivating love and gratitude, (5)awakening wisdom, (6) living ethically, and (7) awakening spiritual vision.

(1) "Transforming motivations" has to do with reducing craving and finding the soul's desire. In the gospel of Luke, Jesus says, "For where your treasure is, there will your heart be also." (12:34). Finding what is most important is surely one of the great challenges of our lives.

(2) "Concentrating and calming the mind" is referred to in every tradition. Centering prayer, meditation, and practices like focusing on the breath to still the thoughts are all examples of the same goal, but from different traditions.

(3) "Selfless service" (or generosity) is the result and the root of compassion, social justice, and all forms of service to the Creation, whether human or not.

(4) "Cultivating love and gratitude" is also described as "cultivating emotional wisdom". My favorite Hindu saint, Ramakrishna, is quoted by Walsh as stating: "The supreme purpose and goal for human life...is to cultivate love". And at least for me, gratitude was rather a natural feeling, which in itself is a blessing.

(5) "Awakening wisdom" seemed like it could not be really practiced, when I read this in the book. But looking at his examples, I see the value of emphasizing what wisdom is and what it is not, and how to search for and uncover it. Wisdom is not intelligence, knowledge, dramatic experiences, or even personal power. It is a thing deeper and more comprehensive than any of these.

(6) "Living ethically" is almost inevitably taught as the foundation of ANY spiritual growth. In every tradition, morality and ethical understanding are the initial doorways into maturity and inner evolution.

(7) "Awakening spiritual vision" has to do with recognizing the sacred in all things. Perhaps the Hindu and indigenous traditions have the most to say about this practice.

The main point of this discussion of Walsh's 7 practices is to illustrate how much agreement there is between world religions in the practices and the goals of the spiritual life. These strivings all help produce a very similar temperament and consciousness in the student of each tradition. The ultimate goal will be described differently, and the awareness of disciples might be as infinitely variable as flakes of snow. But the character and the virtues of the followers will have a great consistency.

Wayne Teasdale's very fine book, *The Mystic Heart,* covers much the same ground, but in a different manner. The subtitle of his book is: *Discovering a Universal Spirituality in the World's Religions.* Instead of detailing his points and arguments, I would say, first, just to read the book yourself! It is a beautiful presentation of many of the themes of this little memoir. Secondly, I would just like to say a few words about his chapter titled, "Natural

Mysticism: Reading the Book of Creation." On page 174 of his book, Teasdale writes:

> *"Natural mysticism is the way of primordial revelation. It unfolds and makes clear the whole realm of the natural world, the mystery of life in all its attributes, and the universe in its entirety. This revelation is ongoing, perennial, and always available to each one of us, in every culture, in every time, in any moment of our lives. It is thus the first and permanent source of revelation."*

To repeat a comment I've already made in another context, this is my experience. Human beings are not above or beyond the natural world and Creation. They are inextricably part of it and are totally interdependent with it. Thus, as Wendell Berry's quote at the beginning of this chapter makes clear, we are dependent upon the land, and it is dependent upon us. The idea of our relationship to this world as having "dominion" (King James Version Bible, Gen. 1:26) is, at best, very one-sided. If humanity remembers the sacred, revelatory nature of the natural world, we will attain a greater harmony with, and sustainable relationship to, the miracle that is the Earth. And it seems that we move toward wisdom in communion with Creation, as we realize a deeper communion with the Greater Reality from which this Creation springs.

We are not bereft of teachers, guides, allies, and mentors. They show up in our lives when we are open to them and make some effort to find them. And one of the critical, necessary lessons humanity has come to learn—much more so than in earlier ages—is our appropriate, harmonious interaction with the Created Order. This absolutely necessary understanding was not so much explicit in the great religions in the past. There was emphasis on individual salvation, on compassion and love to other humans, on enlightenment and expanding consciousness, on social justice, and, "walking humbly with your God." But the care of, and communion with, our mother Earth home was not focused on, or perhaps even understood. Yet now, in my own humble opinion, this inescapable issue has become one of the greatest and most fundamental spiritual challenges of all. Because, for one, we are all caught up in it, rich and poor, Oriental or Occidental, scientific or not, religious or not, even aware or not. It will force us to decide what is more important, clean air and water for everyone, or more material possessions, a greater equality of standards of living, or a polarized world of the haves and have-nots. And of course, a more livable planet, or one which becomes more and more inhospitable, (as Thomas Berry noted in the quote in chapter two of this book), or even hostile to human life. This is, at the core, a spiritual issue for humanity.

In the next and final chapter, I will offer a summing up, and some closing reflections. There are threads running through this little memoir, and I will reiterate a few of them. I hope you will stay with me till the end!

REMEMBRANCE

So softly comes the dawn,
and my friend is slowly dying.

It's not a painful death,
or doesn't seem so,

Just another passing into
the unknown.

And my friend has
not really shown fear,

Has not talked much
about what comes next.

Does not sound too concerned,
and I wonder why?

Maybe the only path for
him is living in the moment,

letting the future take
care of itself.

Not too bad a choice,
when choosing is limited.

Perhaps he has reached
A reconciliation

With his own God,
and so a certain

peace has been granted him,
a feeling that his

life has been worthy,
has not been wasted.

That he has carried out
Some part of his calling.

If that is true,
I hope to be so blessed.

I have loved my friend,
and will still once he has passed,

So when my own day of
transition arrives,

whether at dawn or dusk,
with others or alone,

I will remember my friend,
and hopefully be at ease.

ELEVEN

Last Return to the Memoir
March 2019

M argaret and I live in Colorado now. We moved here in 2017, to be near our son's family. I like the cooler air, the low humidity, and the Rocky Mountains on the horizon. I have found a liberal and compassionate church, Arvada United Methodist, where I sing in the choir. Of course, the UMC denomination has just voted to harden their stance against homosexuality, a sorrowful step backwards. But that is a story for another time.

Almost 20 years ago now, we made the decision to sell the S. Brinson Futch farm in south Georgia. This was not an easy decision for me. I felt—and still feel—very bonded to that land down in Cook County, and to the Futch relatives who still reside there. It was easier for my brother and my mother to let the farm go. None of us had any plan to move back down there. Our cousins who managed the property were getting older and pulling back on all their farming operations. My memories of hunting, fishing, walking with my Dad, and playing with my cousins were all happy ones. Even the small amount of work I did there—harvesting vegetables, working one summer cropping tobacco, sharing decision making after our father passed—was "character building" in my view.

Connection to landscapes, the seasons, the plants and animals that live there, has always been a deep reservoir of grounding for me, as I've indicated in this book. But of course, this land, this farm, this eco-system was the most meaningful of all, coming down to our family from my father's ancestors. Of course, the long, deep history of this place goes back to the Indians who were here long before the whites. Arrowheads recovered from the fields and woods of this area were collected by my cousin, and I marveled at their workmanship, and their evidence of native peoples going far back in time.

We finally made the decision to sell the property to a long-time farm family in the area, an extended clan with three grown sons, and an extensive operation. We did not want to "develop" the land in any way or alter its reality as fields, woodlands, meadows, and wetlands. To a large extent, the new owners have maintained this world. We kept a clause in the sales agreement allowing us to come visit the farm by letting the owners know of our intention. One of the greatest blessings of my life was to spend part of my childhood immersed in that eco-system, and it will live inside me until I pass on.

In our last 10 or 11 years in Austin, I was a member of a United Church of Christ community there—the Congregational Church. This fellowship was, and is, a very progressive, social justice oriented body, and I was very much at home there. I led a couple of classes there, served on various boards, and sang in the choir. One of my very meaningful memories from this church is being able to give a eulogy for a much-loved and respected member of the church, Dr. Mathis Blackstock. Matt and I became friends soon after I came to the church, and he joined the men's group I helped lead. At some point, he learned he was suffering from melanoma, and began to make his plans for his passing. He asked if I would give one of the eulogies, and I was much honored, and said, "Of course." The following is the eulogy I gave in the summer of 2012.

"I first met Dr. Matt Blackstock when I joined the Congregational Church of Austin about six years ago (about 2006). When I was still visiting the church, we struck up a conversation more than once. I came to admire and respect Matt, and we found we had some things in common. He loved nature and music, and so did I. We both had relatives in Georgia. There was also some mutual interest in health care issues, my mother having been a nurse, and there being a doctor or two in my extended family.

Not long after I'd joined the church, Matt approached me about serving on one of the boards of the church, or as the historian. Easygoing as Matt was, he persuaded me to become a deacon. His own love for, and dedication to, the congregation came through in our discussions. Perhaps a year later, another member of the church and I decided to form a men's group, so I announced our intentions in the Sunday service. Matt walked up to me afterwards and said he wanted to be part of the group. We were very happy to have him.

Over the six years that I knew Matt, we had many good conversations. I talked to him at length about his medical career, about family, and about the clinic named for him at Brackenridge Hospital. Matt had a real sense of humor, and I remember several stories from him which made me laugh. He said that in his early years as a GP, there were far fewer specialists. So a family physician like him had to learn some simple surgeries. One of his mentors was showing him a particular procedure, and commented, "Matt, you should never attempt this surgery until you've already performed it twice!" There were quite a few other humorous stories like that, some of which I might not want to relate in polite company.

Some of our conversations focused on spirituality and religion, subjects dear to my own heart. At one point, I asked Matt about prayer. My question went something like this: "Matt, what is your experience of prayer? Do you think anything is happening there?"

And he replied: "I feel like I am being heard." I thought that was a fine answer, so I followed it up, with another inquiry: "So does anything change, or is there a consequence of prayer?" And he said that he felt prayer, first of all, changed him. Whatever else it changed, he wasn't sure. I find these two responses to be both simple and profound. I have to hurry some in my remarks. Matt was very clear in his instructions to me. He said, "Greg, I want this service to keep moving. So keep your comments short—about 5 minutes!"

I'll wrap up these reflections with a short passage which was read at my father's funeral.

From Psalm 116:

"Precious in the sight of the Lord is the death of His saints."

So finally I would say: Fair sailing, Dr. Matt. The world is a better place because of your life and your legacy."

Over the past 25 years, I have officiated at four wonderful wedding ceremonies. The first was in California, at the invitation of my brother-in-law Dominic. The marriage of Beth and Dom (as family calls him) was a joyful and beautiful affair, held in a vineyard near San Luis Obispo. The last ceremony was in Austin, at an old cultural landmark, Threadgill's restaurant. My library co-worker, Monica Jones, asked me to do the honors for her and Josh. It was another delightful day full of happiness and promise.

In between these two ceremonies, I was able to lead the celebration for a niece of ours, Diana Quinlivan, who married Joey Calvano, in a beautiful event in the back yard of relatives in Austin. Their deaf community friends added to the joyous nature of this ceremony, which felt happy and intimate. And the fourth wedding ceremony was for friends of ours, Laura and David Lyon. This was held in a small outdoor chapel in the hill country outside Austin. It was a great honor to help these two fine people seal their covenant with each other. It was a blessing for me as much as it was for them. And there is much love in all four of the families who allowed me to share their hopes and aspirations.

May 2020

I have just passed my 71st birthday. Life seems, as usual, bittersweet. So many blessings, and so much suffering in the world. Just over two years ago, our mother passed away at age 91. This was, of course, an existential milestone for me, and the passing of a generation in our own extended family: she was the last of her siblings to leave this world. Even though I have a certain "blessed assurance" in my life, there is certainly a weariness with the great struggles that seem to never end. I still can't believe Donald Trump was elected President, and his followers do not seem to care what he says or does. Their support does not waver.

July 7, 2020

AND NOW, the Pandemic.

It is called "Covid-19," and believed to have originated in the area of Wuhan, China near the end of 2019. As I write this, the U.S. tops of the list of infections by country. A virus which shows as fever, dry cough, and trouble in breathing. It is in every state, though some, like New York, have stemmed the tide, and monitor it closely for a "second wave."

This country is exhausted and depressed in my view. The divisive, amoral Donald Trump, the virus, then the killing of the black man, George Floyd, by a police officer who kept his knee on Floyd's neck for 8 minutes, all have caused unending anxiety. Protest marches and riots, and white counter-demonstrations went on for a month. Will it change institutional racism in this culture?

Depressed and exhausted. The Fourth of July did not feel celebratory for a great multitude of Americans; rather a time of grieving and sorrow. Two years ago, in my little diary, my feelings were very similar to what they are today (July 3, 2018):

> *"Don't feel patriotic. U.S. going in very dangerous direction. Too many duped by, or playing along with Donald Trump and his enablers.*
>
> *But there is always a Higher Power."*

And for me, who grew up in the white-skin middle class privilege of post WW II America, much of that relatively charmed life has been eroding for some time now. Our culture is so fragmented, our entitled attitudes undermined, our faith in science, reason, and even facts, attacked by Trump and the right-wing echo chamber. It is a very disorienting time to be living in the U.S. Racial strife exacerbated. Economic desperation for millions. And the pandemic stalks our society. Have all the chickens come home to roost? I pray the presidential election in November will replace an administration bent on grievance, white preferences, denial of climate change, and a general rejection of science and any sort of expertise.

The fate of our Mother Earth remains one of my greatest heart-aches. Will the planet shake off a portion of the human beings who are, wittingly or not, causing such damage to the biosphere? We in the developed West are the worst offenders in so many ways. I try to live in the moment, and remember that humans do not have the last word on their own fate, much less the fate of our only home. I remain inspired by the creative people in the world: artists, musicians, poets, and all the others. Even the occasional statesperson!

My sense of Presence never truly goes away, though it does not seem as strong as it has in the past. I think that has more to do with me than the Presence! I work at compassion and justice. My energy is not what it once was, but there is still a lot of vinegar in me. Meeting with a counselor once, I said that sometimes I felt uncomfortable talking about my own suffering when the agonies of others seemed much greater. In so many words, he replied, "Well, there is little suffering, and there is big suffering. All of it is important, and all of it needs attention." That is gospel for now for me.

I mourn for many: young Black men shot and killed for no defensible reason; children abused early in their lives, and innocence withers; all those suffering mental and emotional illness, and all those who have given up hope and live a robotic life. Thin skin? Bleeding heart? I think not. "Nothing human can be alien to me" is a paraphrase of the Roman Terence. "As you do it unto the least of these, you do it unto me," said Jesus. Boundaries are necessary through life. But so is living beyond them.

We lose so much in this life. What is it that is *not* lost?

TWELVE

Closing Thoughts

"The door is always open, for those who love the prophets."

This was spoken by the Sufi teacher I had come to hear. The words were uttered to me and a couple of other folks as he walked up to us after his formal teaching. One by one, he shook our hands, and we felt the blessing of his attention and his presence. This Sufi master uttered a perennial truth. The door of awakening, the door of growth, the door of transformation, is always open to those who seek it out. "Seek and ye shall find," said Jesus, and the import is the same.

The healing of Mother Earth, the maturing of human individuals, and the raising of consciousness in general: all these truths are inextricably entwined. This is not a fantasy, or denial of complex realities, not ignorance of the dark side of human affairs and the human heart. Instead, one's own growth is intimately tied to the possibility of healing and growth in the world at large. And vice versa!

There are no guarantees. Perhaps humanity will go through some global traumas (possibly fearsome die-offs in population) before a turn toward a healthier, sustainable culture and lifestyle is realized. Homo sapiens may even face extinction. Nothing in the history and the biology of our planet could rule that out. But, at least for myself, and I know many others, there is an awareness and an experience of Something timeless and ultimately benevolent upholding and maintaining all of Reality. The profound beauty of this world, and the majesty of the human heart are reflections of this same ineffable Mystery. Each person must decide for themselves if this is true.

I hope that the reader has been able to get some feeling for why I sub-titled this work *A Memoir as a Meditation.* My pervasive awareness has been of my life being a "wrestling with the Spirit." A constant pull of the Ineffable has acted on me, usually even without my consciousness. Often, I have doubted it; and at times, even fought against it. But there is no denying it in my heart and soul. Much of the writing here is a reflection and meditation on my own experience. And the love of our Earth-home is fundamental to that experience.

Our treatment of the natural world is absolutely linked to our greater awareness and deepening wisdom. These qualities cannot be nurtured without an openness to them, a desire to see them grow within us. One must first desire them, and as Rumi teaches in the quote opening the book, one must, "Ask for what you really want." The Universe will respond to this yearning. It may not be easy, and in fact, usually isn't. But it is the way toward, "Peace that passeth understanding."

I appreciate and respect those readers who have stayed with me in this reflection. I hope it has offered some inspiration, some challenge, even some revelation. Every individual has a story to tell. I believe each story has import and hidden treasures for those who can discover them. Peace be with you, and I hope you will allow the Universe to guide you.

AMEN

"Neither death nor life"

(Paul the Apostle)

Late afternoon, heading toward dusk,
a bit cool in this Colorado first week of Spring.

Slight breeze thru pines and fir,
slow fading sunlight.

Calm on my own in this
time of pandemic,

as this lovely natural world is
like it ever was

for me, always comforting in scent,
sound, and sight

In and of and thru it,
the sense of Presence continues
in my awareness.

Through no merit of
my own. Just the same
feeling since childhood,

Almost an impersonal Love,
but love, nonetheless.

Fear, anger, even panic
near surface and in the
eyes of some.

151

Yet my own journey,
   inner and outer,
      has this steady Pulse.

Through memory of past,
   and imagination of future,

through friends and family,
   even in strangers, even in
      the lost

This Companion so recurring,
   whether called Self in the
      East, Holy Spirit in the West,

Nameless to ones who don't
   want labels.

My praise and gratitude
   come out before words.

Sun is lower, just a bit
   cooler on this bench.

Don't know if this Creation
   gave the feeling first, or

I felt the Presence, then
saw it reflected in Mother Earth.

My heart is full, even
   in the face of this frightening
      Unknown,

Praise to YOU,
   Holy One, Whatever
      and Whoever YOU ARE.

3/22/2020

PERMISSIONS and REFERENCES

I have been blessed by the many authors and representatives who have graciously given permissions for the quotes I have included. I am humbled by the willingness of these people to let me use words that have taught and touched me. In particular, Coleman Barks, Wendell Berry, and Richard Rohr were so kind in their responses to someone who was unknown to them. I also laughed with joy, at the Swami whose name I did not get, answering from a Vedanta center in California, regarding the Ramakrishna quote, who said: "Oh no, no permission needed!" Peace be with them all.

1. Coleman Barks, Rumi quote as epigraph at front of book, *The Essential Rumi,* p. 36; Harper, San Francisco, 1995.

2. Wendell Berry, quote from *Our Only World,* p. 111; Counterpoint, Berkeley, 2015.

3. Ibn Arabi, quote from *Kernel of the Kernel,* by Ismail Hakki Bursevi, translated by Bulent Rauf; Beshara Publications, 2016.

4. Ramakrishna, quote from *Sayings of Sri Ramakrishna,* p. 149, Sri Ramakrishna Math, Chennai, 1971.

5. Wayne Teasdale quote from the book *The Mystic Heart.* Copyright © 1999 by Wayne Teasdale. Reprinted with permission of New World Library, Novato, CA. www.newworldlibrary.com.

6. Thomas Berry, quote from *The Dream of the Earth,* p.2, Sierra Club Books, San Francisco, 1988.

7. Bill Plotkin, *Soulcraft,* p. 1. New World Library, Novato, CA 2003.

8. "Bluebird" poem and the review of *Soulcraft* were printed first in "The Ecozoic Reader", Vol 3, #4 (2003), and Vol. 4, #4 (2007), respectively.

9. Richard Rohr, *Falling Upward,* p. 74, Jossey-Bass, San Francisco, 2011

10. Don Saliers, *The Soul in Paraphrase,* p.11, Seabury Press, 1980

11. Fred Craddock, *As One Without Authority,* p. 59, Abingdon, Nashville, 1981

ACKNOWLEGEMENTS

There will be far too many people and groups to thank in a limited space. The following is my good-faith effort. First I would like to mention the folks who have read at least one of my chapters, and some who have read many or all of them. Listing them here does not mean they necessarily agreed with what I wrote, or even share my worldview. However, they all have given me important feedback, (even if they do not remember doing so). The list includes: Dr. Sarah Jackson, Rev. Sid Hall, Dr. Don Saliers, Rev. Dan Wilson, Dr. Will Taegel, Sidney Futch, Ronnie Futch, Dr. Bill Plotkiin, Rev. Jo Jensen, Troy Jakobeit, Rev. Sharon McCormick, Bonnie O'Connell, Ron Baxendale.

I would also like to mention the communities that have nurtured and guided my spiritual journey and my emotional growth—aside from my families of origin. Two churches in particular come to mind, both are Trinity churches—Trinity UMC in Atlanta, and Trinity Church in Austin. Other communities include: the Congregational Church of Austin, the Earthtribe community of Texas, my Austin Public library community, and the men's group in Austin, which still going strong for at least 15 years.

My wife of over 45 years(!), Margaret, has been a gift to many people, especially the kids of her Montessori classrooms, her grandkids, and her son, Matthew, and to me! She is a fine watercolor artist, and a voracious reader.

Of course, I could not have written this work without the consistent support and guidance of my editor, Mindy Reed, and her helpers at the Authors' Assistant, including Rebecca Byrd Arthur. Mindy is a long-time Austin Public library stalwart, and her establishment of the Recycled Reads store in Austin is an accomplishment admired across the library world. I highly recommend her to any aspiring authors!

My dear readers, allow me to add one more acknowledgement: the Great Mystery, the Holy One, the Ultimate Reality which (WHO) has guided and supported me since childhood. Praise be unto You, Nameless One, and accept my eternal gratitude.

Made in the USA
Columbia, SC
19 September 2022

66704542R00088